LIFE IN CORNWALL
1943 – 1946

EXTRACTS FROM
THE WEST BRITON NEWSPAPER

PHOTOGRAPHS FROM
THE ELLIS COLLECTION

TEXT SELECTED AND EDITED BY
CATHARINE INCE

COUNTRY BOOKS

Published by Country Books
Courtyard Cottage, Little Longstone, Bakewell, Derbyshire DE45 1NN
Tel: 01629 640670
Email: dickrichardson@country-books.co.uk
www.countrybooks.biz

ISBN 978-1-906789-74-9

ACKNOWLEDGEMENTS

My thanks to the editor of the *West Briton* for letting me use extracts from the paper, and to the advertisers, where they could be traced. I am very grateful to Kim Cooper and her staff of the Cornish Studies Library, Redruth, for all their help and forbearance. To Caroline Gillatt for proofreading, and to Martin Buck and Trish Roberts for help with my inexperience of computers, and to my publsher, Dick Richardson, for his help and patience.

THE PHOTOGRAPHS

Most of the illustrations are taken from the Ellis Collection held at the Cornish Studies Library in Redruth. It consists of about 112,000 images, with mostly glass plate negatives, taken by George Ellis, during the period 1939 – 1980. He had been a freelance newspaper photographer working in Fleet Street, London, before the war and moved to Cornwall at the outbreak of war. He also photographed many weddings, babies, local happenings as well as local news items, mostly in the area of Bodmin and St. Austell. The collection was purchased by Cornwall County Council and is perhaps, the most important single collection of images held in Cornwall.

The other three photographs were taken from the collection of The Poly Local History and Research Group, Falmouth, for which I thank them

Unfortunately the West Briton did not keep the actual photographs that were printed in the paper and the illustrations on microfiche are not very clear.

Printed and bound in England by 4edge Ltd., Hockley, Essex

DEDICATION

This book is dedicated to the memory of my sister Alison 1941 – 2007.

THE EDITOR

CATHARINE INCE came to Cornwall in September 1941 with her parents and younger sister when her father was appointed as the first full time consultant obstetrician and gynaecologist in the county. After trying two of the local private schools, she was sent to Kingsley School, which had been evacuated from London to Tintagel for the duration of the war. She has tried various jobs – horticulture, dairying, milk testing, before settling down to primary school teaching, mostly in Cornwall. She spent a year in New South Wales, Australia, on a teachers' exchange, visiting Moonta, South Australia, known as "Australia's Little Cornwall."

She now does some voluntary work but her first love is her dogs. She has bred and shown them in the past, starting in 1961, off and on, until the last few years. She has gone back to her first love, Manchester Terriers, but now keeps two as pets only. She was quoted as one of the world's leading authorities on the breed when she contributed the chapter on the breed in *The World Encyclopaedia of Dogs*.

TABLE OF WEIGHTS, MEASUREMENTS AND MONEY

2 ounces (ozs.)	= 57 grams approx.
16 oz. =1 pound (lb.)	= 453 grams approx.
14 lbs.	= 1 stone
2·2lbs.	= 1 kilogram approx.
12 inches (ins.)	= 1 foot (ft.)
3 ft.	=1 yard
39·5 ins. approx.	= 1 metre
1760 yards	= 1 mile
20 fluid ounces	= 1 pint
8 pints	= 1 gallon
1 pint	= 568 mls approx.
1·76 pints	= 1 litre
¼ penny (d.)	= 1 farthing (4 farthings to 1 penny)
½d	= 1 halfpenny (ha'penny)
12d.	= 1 shilling (1/-) = 5p
2/6d	= half a crown
20 shillings	= £1 = 100p
21 shillings	= 1 guinea
Notes in general use:	10/-, £1 and £5
Coins in general use:	¼d, ½d, 1d, 3d, 6d, 1/-, 2/-, 2/6d.

Note
The use of italics in the main text are for summaries, and that after the date of publication, additional information.

INTRODUCTION

This book, it is hoped, will jog the memories of those of us that lived through the war years, and explain to those of us who were not born a little of how life was lived in those days. It is, as it has to be, a purely personal choice of articles, which appeared in the *West Briton*, or to give it its full title, *The West Briton and Cornwall Advertiser*. The book is not meant to be read from cover to cover but dipped into!

The paper was, and still is, read all over the world and is known as the "Cornishman's Bible". During the war, births, deaths, marriages, sports results, garden fetes, Women's Institutes meetings, church and chapel meetings, for sale and wanted, local auctions, what's on at the cinema, etc., were the backbone of the paper. There was no National Health Service – doctors and hospitals had to be paid for by the patient or by some form of insurance or by the Public Assistance Board for those who could not pay. Workhouses had been replaced, in name only, by the Public Assistance Institutes. The death penalty was the ultimate deterrent to crime. The Old Age Pension for a single person in 1939 was 10/- a week (50p) which is less than the cost of the *West Briton* today. Gas was produced in the towns from coal and stored in a gasometer, but it was only available in the town. Many houses, especially in the countryside, still used oil lamps and candles and many others still had outdoor toilets, often just a hole in the ground or a bucket! Central heating and double glazing were almost unknown, micro-wave ovens and superstores had yet to be thought of, black and white television was in its infancy and only available in certain areas of London. Telephones were scarce. The price of the paper was 2d on Thursdays and 1d for Monday's Truro edition.

During the war there were a great many activities which were suppressed by the Government and did not appear in the papers – where the bombs fell, where the R.A.F. stations were, the use of seaports, especially Falmouth, Penzance and Newlyn and what went on there, the work of the police, the Home Guard, the A.R.P. personnel. For local books on these subjects I would recommend Viv Acton and Derek Carter's *Operation Cornwall 1940-1944* and also their *War and Peace*.

In the 1930's fewer people had cameras and films during the war were almost un-obtainable to the public and, because so many places were out of bounds, very few photographs exist today. The *West Briton* is only available on microfilm and the quality of the images is not good, so I have been fortunate in being able to access the Ellis Collection to illustrate this book.

By 1943 the tide of war was beginning to turn and the Americans had joined the war. Food rationing and clothing coupons were here to stay well into peace time, and furniture was difficult to buy. War Savings groups sprang up everywhere, to lend money to the Government to help war effort. Gardens fetes, horse and dog shows were curtailed, Young Farmers Clubs, were organised to assist the Red Cross, Prisoners of War, and many other groups with funds. Towns and organisations competed to raise money to buy aeroplanes, tanks and ammunition. The *West Briton* also began listing local servicemen, sometimes with photographs, those that were prisoners, that had died and those that were missing.

There was still no National Health Service. Bread was still unrationed until after the war but the queues at food shops, butchers, bakers, grocers, greengrocers, were getting longer and the food scarcer. After the end of the war in 1945 it took many years to get back to the standards of pre-war Britain.

1943

Chinese Girl At Helston

A young Chinese girl, Diana Wong, is visiting Helston to tell the story of her country's great resistance to the Japanese invader. Miss Wong was born in Malaya. She was educated in England, and has appeared in several films and West End productions. Her films include *Broken Blossoms*, *Chinese Bungalow*, and *Things To Come*. Before the war she intended to finish training at Sorbonne, Paris. She was caught by the Nazi invasion and was forced to flee to England. Her father is still in Malay and probably a Japanese prisoner. She will address a meeting arranged by the Ministry of Information at Godolphin Hall, Helston, at 7.15 p.m., on January 20th.   14/1/1943

Killed By Machine Gun

One of the victims of an air raid on the South-West, on Sunday, was a native of Falmouth, Mr. Jim Skinner. He and his wife were killed by machine gun fire when they were on their way to the railway station to return to their home. A writer in the Royal Navy, Mr. Skinner, aged 37, was the eldest son of Mr. and Mrs. Sydney J. Skinner, of Wodehouse-terrace, Falmouth, and he followed in his father's footsteps as a Rugby player, was selected to take part in Cornwall Rugby trials, and also Plymouth Albion. Before joining the forces he was on the Bath staff of Westminster Bank.   14/1/1943

Mr. W. Lewis of Lostwithiel, aged 90, who carries on his shoe repairing business.   *13/1/1943*

Council Sell Farm – Proceeds To Pay For A New Cemetery

Gwennap Parish Council will lose the distinction of being probably the only authority of its kind in the country to own a freehold farm, when it acts on a resolution, approved by ten votes to two at a sparsely-attended parish meeting in Cusgarne Council School, on Thursday, to sell the property by public action and devote the proceeds as directed by the Ministry of Health… as conditions prevailing in the existing cemetery at Church-town were absolutely deplorable.   21/1/1943

The farm was a house, out buildings, and 20 acres at Trebost, Stithians, which was eventually sold for £1,460.

Advertisement

M.B.E. For Gallant Falmouth Man

The King has been pleased to approve the award of M.B.E. (Civil Division) to Gilbert Brodie, third engineer officer, and Eric George Booth, seventh engineer officer, of the Merchant Navy. Mr. Booth is a Falmouth man, whose home is at 8, Clifton-terrace. The ship in which he was serving was sailing alone, and was subjected to three U-boat attacks which caused extensive damage. The first attack was made in day-light and the enemy was immediately engaged by the defensive armament. After the third torpedo had struck the ship it was thought that she was sinking and the engines were stopped. The Master, Capt. P. Johnston, of South Shields, who is awarded the O.B.E., decided to make an attempt to save her, and the third and seventh engineer officers volunteered to return to the engine room to start the main engines. This courageous action, undertaken with the full knowledge that the submarine was still in the vicinity and that they would stand little chance if the vessel was hit again, made possible the saving of the vessel. The Master displayed courage and skill in beating off the enemy and, by his determination and resource, brought his crippled ship to port. Mr. Booth, who is 23, is the son of the late Mr. A. Booth, and Mrs. Booth, was educated at Wellington-terrace and the Day Continuation Schools, Falmouth. He served his apprenticeship with Messrs. Silley, Cox and Co., Ltd., and went to sea about two years ago. He was formerly captain of the Docks Apprentices Cricket Club. His three brothers are serving in the Navy.   21/1/1943

Food Facts – Extra EGGS And MILK

Lots of things are new in this war. We've learnt to make omelettes without breaking eggs. We've discovered that Household Milk is a great help when liquid milk is short. We must make use of these dried foods because they save millions of tons of shipping. And remember, they've grand food value. Each package of dried Egg equals 12 shell eggs, yet costs only 1/9d. Each tin of Household Milk makes four pints of milk – milk with all the goodness except the fat – at 9d. a tin.

Issued by The Ministry of Food.   28/1/1943

Platoon 21 C Company, Bodmin Barracks.   *23/1/1943*

Advertisement

German Moored Mines

The Ministry of Home Security states that German moored mines have recently been found in a state which renders them dangerous when adrift and liable to detonate when they reach the shore. If, therefore, a floating mine is seen about to strand itself, persons on the shore should at once inform the police, who will take the necessary steps to evacuate the area.   4/2/1943

To Prevent Flower Smuggling

An amending regulation, the Press Association understands, will be issued shortly which have the effect of preventing the continuance of flower smuggling traffic by rail from Cornwall. Since the ban on transport by train came into force, people have been getting round the regulation by bringing flowers disguised as personal luggage, and selling them in London.   11/2/1943

Mr. Tom Brown, of Port Isacc, preparing lobster pots for the new season. *16/2/1943*

Wonderful West Powder Record

"I think that the best report I have ever heard presented here" commented the Chairman, (Mr. F.R. Pascoe)…at the West Powder Licensing Sessions at Truro on Saturday. *There were no convictions for drunkeness.* There had been one case of drunkenness since 1939 – a female evacuee – and that could not be attributed to the fault of the licensee as the liquor was consumed outside the licensed premises. Mr. Pascoe :- I think I almost ought to be presented with a pair of white gloves. It is a wonderful report… All the licences will be renewed. 18/2/1943

Fell Over Coal Plat – Action Against Portreath Company Fails

An action transferred from Cornwall Assizes, was heard by Mr. Justice Lawrence, at Devon Assizes, on Tuesday. The plaintiff, Sergt. Edmund Jones, R.A.F., of Grays, Essex, sought to recover damages from the Beynon Shipping Co., Ltd., Portreath, in respect of injuries received at Portreath on March 23rd. 1941, when he fell over a coal plat belonging to defendants… Plaintiff's case was that he fell over a wall at Harbour-terrace into a coal plat, and fractured his spine. It was alleged that the coal plat was a nuisance and dangerous and that defendants had wrongfully permitted or caused the dumping place to be opening on to the highway without any fence or railings, or giving warning that it was dangerous to persons lawfully passing along the highway. Plaintiff fell 15ft… Dismissing the claim, with costs, the Judge found that the coal plat was not a nuisance and not dangerous.

At this time Portreath Harbour was used by coal boats and the area around the harbour was used to store coal until it was collected by lorries or horse and cart. 18/2/1943

Dolcoath Shaft Headgear Dismantled

A notable landmark in Camborne-Redruth area has disappeared in consequence of the dismantling, last week, of the massive iron headgear which for years stood in idleness over the new Dolcoath mine at Roskear, Camborne. The huge plant, one of the largest headgears ever erected in Cornwall, was first built many years ago over the new Williams shaft at Pengegon… The iron will now be utilised in furtherance of the war effort.   25/2/1943

Repaid Kindness – By Gift Of Stolen Batteries

"These women had been kind to me and I wanted to repay their kindness. I didn't mean to get them into any trouble", said Horace Carr, residing at 20, Church-street, Helston, who was fined £1 at Pydar Petty Sessions, St. Columb, on Tuesday, for stealing two 120-volt batteries, valued 14s.6d. He pleaded guilty. It was stated that he gave the batteries to two women about three or four months ago. They did not know the batteries were not his property. They had told him they could not get any batteries for their wireless sets. He did not receive anything for either of the batteries.   25/2/1943

Confiscated Flowers

The wards of the Royal Cornwall Infirmary, the County Isolation Hospital, and the children's hostel at Redruth have been gaily decorated with flowers this week. Few, if any, of the patients who enjoy their brightness knew how they came to be there. "Flower Racketeers" are gradually being rounded up, but some are still prepared to run the gauntlet in trying to transport flowers to big town markets. *Many suit-cases contain flowers and one racketeer had three sacks with him with lettuce on top but anemones and violets*

Mrs. Smith of Treknow, Tintagel who helped collect paper salvage on her bicycle raising £150. She was unable to use her car owing to petrol rationing.   *26/2/1943*

underneath. The value of the flowers was estimated to be £35. The County Isolation Hospital at St. Clements, Truro, has now been turned into apartments.   25/2/1943

Flowers Sent By Sea

An experiment in transporting flowers by sea, now that carriage by road or rail is banned, has proved a "great success", according to Mr. F.C. Saltmarsh, a Liverpool fruiterer. A ship carrying about 1,600 boxes (five train wagon loads) arrived at Liverpool recently, and street flower-sellers had daffodils, violets, anemones, and narcissi to offer. The ship was in ballast, so the flowers did not interfere with the war effort.   4/3/1943

Advertisement

Gas Helps To Sooth And Sweeten Life
Save Gas for the Factories!

The Gas Industry provides the Nation with more than gas for cooking, warming and other household needs. From the by-products of gas-making — tar, coke, benzole, ammonia and sulphur — a thousand and one articles are made for war and civil use. The aspirin that soothes your head-aches and the saccharin that sweetens your war-time tea are made from benzole. So are explosives, aviation spirit, dyes, printing inks and paints and varnishes used for camouflage. From tar comes plastics, creosote, disinfectants and many other products vital in war and peace; and from ammonia we get fertilisers and explosives; from sulphur, valuable industrial acids. The Gas Industry also helps in the Battle for Fuel by providing half a ton of coke from every ton of coal used in the gas works. But although more gas and by-products are needed for war purposes, gas-manufacturing plant is not elastic; there is a limit to the amount of gas that can be made in a given time.

Do Your Share By Saving More Gas.   4/3/1943

Gas was produced in every town by burning coal in a retort boiler, the gas given off was then stored in a gasometer and piped to homes and industry in the immediate vicinity.

They Will Run Without Petrol

It is proposed to adapt 46 more Western National 'buses to producer gas in 1943. The Tilling group aim at converting 651 in all during the present year. Already they have adapted 107, including 14 Western National, and these have run 2,500,000 miles, so saving 415,000 gallons of imported fuel.   4/3/1943

By Pigeon Post

The hon. secretaries of local Savings Committees in Cornwall have received by pigeon post messages from Lord Kindersley, President of the National Savings Committee, who released 1,300 pigeons in Trafalgar-square, on Saturday. Lord Kindersley's message ran:- "On this opening day of the Wings for Victory Campaign, I send you and your committee this winged messenger with greetings and good wishes for your effort. May victory come to us on wings which you will help provide".   11/3/1943

Teams Of Cyclists

Despite the ban on long-distance transport of flowers by rail, spring blooms from the Cornish Riviera are reaching London in small quantities. They are travelling quite legitimately by the strangest method ever. Teams of stout-hearted cyclists, working in

Children of Tredeth Sick Bay for Evacuees picking daffodils at Helland Bridge, little Bertha in front.
13/3/1943

relays, are pedalling them all the way and some of the flowers have covered between 250 and 300 miles before they reach Covent Garden. Wild rumours as to the amount these cyclists are earning are being circulated in London. One report says they are making £20 a week, but enquiries in the market suggest that this is a gross exaggeration, though wholesalers in the market agree that the cyclists are being well paid for their labours.
18/3/1943

Daffodils 3d A Bunch
Cornish flower growers expect that daffodils will be threepence a bunch in London tomorrow (Friday). To-day the first train since the removal of the ban on transport left Penzance with consignments for London and the provinces, and it is feared that the market may be flooded. During the restrictions, daffodils fetched as much as £1 a bunch in London.
25/3/1943

32-Year-Old Cob Follows Master's Coffin
The death occurred at Lambourne, Penhallow, of Mr. Thomas Northcott, aged 97. He was the youngest son of Mr. Barnabas Northcott, of Meudan, Mawnan, where he was born. He came to Lambourne in about 1860… Until the age of 95, Mr. Northcott worked actively on the farm, and rode horseback regularly. He was always an admirer of a good

horse, he is survived by his old cob, which, at the age of 32, is still doing useful work, tilling the land for Mr. Reynolds, at Ventongimps…By request of Mr. Northcott, the coffin was drawn on a farm wagon by an old cart horse owned by Mr. J.P. Tredinnick, and was followed by his old cob, Charlie.   25/3/1943

Advertisement

No – Coupon Dairy Farm

Forty-five dairy cows and heifers have come through the winter on a 65-acre dairy farm in Cornwall, without any purchased feeding-stuffs. And the farmer, Mr. E.J. Crowle, Coldharbour Dairy Farm, Bodmin, intends to carry on without resorting to coupons…

Liskeard "Wings For Victory" indicator board, unveiled by Mayor Alderman W. H. Huddy. 6/4/1943

One cow gave 1,000 gallons of milk in six winter months and 2,000 in her lactation. *He grew hay which he cut in June last, then he cut a second clover cut for silage, he grew beans, peas, vetches and oats for silage, sowing the crops at intervals to cut young. Oats, beans, spring wheat to provide winter production rations, linseed for the heaviest milkers and for rearing calves. In the autumn he fed marrow-stemmed kale. Coupons were allocated to buy in food stuffs.* 1/4/1943

American Hustle

Surveyors, architects, and members of the building trade in Cornwall were immensely interested in a talking film depicting a record-breaking feat in the United States, where 5,000 houses for dock workers were erected in five months… All stages in the precision-built pre-fabricated houses were shown, and the film illustrated how building can be speeded up to meet war-time conditions. The subject is of universal interest at the moment… There is a shortage of five million houses in this country, and after the war the building industry would be fully occupied upon reconditioning buildings which had been damaged by enemy action to make them again habitable.   8/4/1943

Took Material From Grounded Barrage Balloon

"When there is Government property anywhere about the public should understand that they must not help themselves to it", said the Chairman, at a Westcountry police court, yesterday, when George Isaacs, Sidney Hendy, and Alfred Dunn were summoned for removing part of a deflated barrage balloon. All three defendants pleaded guilty… A barrage balloon grounded and on reaching the ground it became deflated. The salvage staff were unable to collect the balloon until five days later. By then nearly all the material had been taken away. The portions were recovered from the three men and from 30 boys in the area… The approximate value of a barrage balloon was estimated in Warships was £500 to £700… Defendants were fined 5s each.   8/4/1943

Home News For N. Africa

In a letter received by Mr. and Mrs. E. Juleff, Churchtown, Summercourt, their son, driver S. Juleff, R.A.S.C., serving in North Africa, writes that the *West Briton* arrives every week without fail, and is greatly appreciated by himself and the other Cornish lads in the company. As one finishes it, it is passed on to another, until it is read by about a dozen.
15/4/1943

Dangerous Practice

"It was a very dangerous thing to go around the county with a big lorry and no lights at all", commented the Chairman (Mr. F.R. Pascoe), at West Powder Police Court, at Truro, on Saturday, when William John Coad, of Callestick, was fined £2 and ordered to pay 1s 9d. costs for driving a lorry without lights. Defendant pleaded guilty. *He stated that it had been moonlight and his lights had failed.*   15/4/1943

Cost Of Rats

Ten shillings a year is the average price paid by a farmer for the food and board of each rat on his farm, one pair of rats and their offspring can produce 880 rats in a year. Neither the farmer nor the nation can afford to lose food and feeding stuffs to the value of more than £25 million a year. These four-legged U-boats are not a secret weapon designed by Hitler, but their effects on demands for shipping space make them an important part of his submarine warfare. Every ton of food denied the rats means another ton of weapons to be used against the Axis.   22/4/1943

St. Ives driving class at the show. *24/4/1943*

The Axis was an alliance of Germany and Italy formed before and during the Second World War, later extended to include Japan.

Falmouth Is Out For £120,000
Scholars of the secondary, elementary and private schools at Falmouth have set themselves to raise £5,000, the cost of a Typhoon, as part of the borough's Wings for Victory Week savings drive from May 22nd to 28th… Falmouth's target is £120,000 for a Sunderland, five Beaufighters, and six Spitfires. 24/4/1943

Most Original Fisherman
Ask any fisherman in Coverack to-day who is the most original fisherman, and he will say Alec Symes, twenty-one-year-old Merchant navy seaman, native of Coverack. Lying face down, and with the aid of a water glass and spear, he patiently waits until a large plaice glides into the more peaceful waters surrounding the pier. "Wind and tide both must be taken into consideration", he explained to a *West Briton* representative. Body taut, eyes firmly fixed on a target deep under the water, he carefully aims the spear. A false move to the left or right may mean a wasted day. Caught unawares, the surprised victim is his. "I first thought of the idea of spearing fish this way while serving at sea", he said. "You see, the glass, which has copper sides, does not magnify the fish under the water, but enables me to see through the water. Even if the sea is rough, it will smooth it out, revealing any fish underneath. All the same, it is an art and needs constant practice". His last success was on a day when fish was difficult to obtain. On this occasion his catch was an extra large plaice. Having been bombed twice at while at sea, he is waiting to join a ship, ready to continue a different type of sea-fight – against the Hun. 6/5/1943

St. Merryn Aerodrome – teaching aircraft recognition of a Heinkel.   *24/4/1943*

Correspondence – Pasties And Rationing

Sir – I should be much obliged if Mr. W.E. Rowe, of Kerrier Rural Council, would let country housewives know how he manages to live only on his rations. I should like to know if he lives in town or country, as the townsfolk have great advantages of buying unrationed food, going to restaurants for meals, and also fish and chips, thus saving their rations for a weekend. If the housewives had more fat allowance they would not trouble much about pasties, and, seeing it is a Government scheme, why should Mr. Rowe worry? If Mr. Rowe does hard manual labour, and does not keep poultry, go out for meals or keep a farm, and lives only on his points and ration allowances he is very patriotic. Thank goodness he is not Lord Woolton.

H. Prynn. Trenoweth Barton, Grampound Road.   13/5/1943

The Great Gale

One of the severest gales experienced in Cornwall for many years raged during the week-end, and, in addition to doing damage to crops and fruit blossom, it left the young greens of the trees and hedges brown or almost blackened, as though a great fire had swept over the countryside. Heavy rain set in on the evening of Friday,
May 7th, with the wind rising to gale force. During 24 hours 1·47 ins. of rain was recorded, and nearly half of it fell in one hour. The gale, which was cold and cutting, was westerly and the maximum mean hourly velocity was 42 miles an hour on the Saturday morning, rising to gusts of about 70 miles an hour.   20/5/1943

Bodmin "Wings For Victory" target indicator.   *26/5/1943*

Proud Of Her "Dam Buster" Grandson

One of the proudest women in Cornwall is Mrs. E. Strike, of Parc-an-Cairn, Porthleven, widow of Capt. Edward Strike, late of the Hain Steamship Company, whose grandson, Wing Commander Guy Gibson, R.A.F., double D.S.O. and double D.F.C., led the force of Lancaster bombers which wrought such widespread havoc following their attack on Germany's greatest dams, the Mohne and Eder.   20/5/1943

Guy Gibson was later awarded the Victoria Cross for his part in the bursting of the Ruhr Dam.

Correspondence – Ice Cream

Sir – I see in the *West Briton* that Lostwithiel Food Committee are afraid that lots of dried milk is liable to go bad owing to the fact that there is little demand for it. All this powder could be used if the ban on ice cream was lifted for the summer months. It seems unfair that a total ban is placed on ice cream, which used to be the greatest luxury a child could get for a penny. Not only from the point of the consumer, but also several small shops used to rely on the sale of ices during the summer months to help them over the winter.

Yours truly, Irene Hawes. 7, Colinsey-place, Penzance.   27/5/1943

Nest In Overcoat Pocket

Despite the noise of the smithy and all the sparks flying from the hot metal being shaped by Mr. Alfred Tamblyn, in his blacksmith's shop at Probus, a wren chose a pocket of an overcoat hanging near the big fire in which to build her nest. She hatched her brood and fed them, and took them on their first flight last Friday.   10/6/1943

The Czech Spirit

An exhibition of Czechoslovak art, composed of a selection of pictures by soldier artists and other contemporary painters, is to open free to the public all this week at the art gallery and museum of the Royal Institution of Cornwall, Truro. When it was opened by Lord Clifdon on Saturday the suggestion was made that after the war the collection, on its return to Prague, might be given a separate gallery as a reminder of the link which had been forged between Cornwall and Czechoslovakia by the exhibition.   10/6/1943

Children Destroyed Falmouth's Banana Tree

… *Falmouth Town Council* had been fortunate enough to grow a banana tree in the open, and it had four bananas ripening. These were to have been auctioned for the British Red Cross Fund. Although the tree was fenced with wire-netting, children, with sticks smashed it to pieces. *The Town Council* was loathed to bring the children before a Juvenile Court, but an example would have to be made of future offenders. 10/6/1943

Two Bottles Of Brandy Produce £3,950

Two bottles of brandy sold by auction by Mr. Hugo Rowe at an open-air boxing match at Penryn, last evening, in connection with Penryn "Wings for Victory" Week, produced £3,950. Each bottle was sold and re-sold three times, the prices paid being £1,250, £1,000, and £800 (first bottle), £500, £250 and £150, a condition being that the purchaser agreed to invest in War Savings the amout of his purchase price.   10/6/1943

His First Visit To St. Ives

Born at Madron, and working on a farm only six miles from St. Ives, Mr. Albert Matthews, of Zennor, visited St. Ives for the first time. A farm labourer, Mr. Matthews, who is 67 years of age, served in France during the last war. Mr. Matthews said "This is my first visit to St. Ives, but I am coming again. I have been to Sennen, but not as far as The Lands End".   10/6/1943

Minister On Horseback

The bi-centenary of the first visit of the Wesleys to Cornwall is to be celebrated at Pool, on July 17th, when the Rev. W.H. Brackenbury, the local Methodist minister, is to ride a horse through the main street. The celebration will be in the nature of a reconstruction of John Wesley's visit, when he arrived on horseback and preached to the miners, using a large, flat stone as a pulpit. The stone is now in a a farm near Carn Brea Railway Station, and it is the intention of Mr. Brackenbury to lead a short service from the same spot. 17/6/1943

Cow Goes For A Dip

A cow belonging to Mr. A.W. Matthews, Mousehole, ran out of the fold, on Tuesday, through the village, over the rocks, and swam out to sea beyond the island. Men took a boat and, with the help of a crew of a local motor boat, the cow was brought to land. Before it could be got in a lorry it had given its captors an anxious time.   17/6/1943

Baby Found In Cornfield

Hearing a baby crying, Mr. W.J. Anstis, of Treyew Farm, Truro, on Monday evening, went into a cornfield at Highertown and there he found the child, which had been placed in a cardboard box and abandoned. It was a boy about three weeks old, fairly well

Bodmin – County School boys leaving to pick potatoes at Penzance.   *19/6/1943*

Newquay Horse Show – Mr. C.R. Richards, Splatton Ridden, Lelant, with Ann and her foal, Best Horse in Show. *26/6/1943*

dressed and nourished. There were no means of identification. The police are making enquiries. 24/6/1943

The mother was later found in Plymouth following a description given of a woman seen carrying a box on the day of the discovery of the baby near where he was found. She was charged with abandoning the baby in a manner likely to cause it unnecessary suffering. She stated that the father of the child was not her husband.

How They Escaped From Their Axis Captors

A grand masquerade in a gaily-coloured coach from the palace of the Bey of Tunis helped a St. Ives Merchant Navy skipper and a friend to escape from their Axis captors. Captain William Richard Williams, son of the late Mr. and Mrs. John Williams, of Carbis Valley, and a nephew of Mrs. Ben Rowe, of Hillside Villas, Carbis Bay, was the skipper. Capt. Williams, who now resides at Cardiff, was awarded the D.S.O. in 1941, and was recently invested at Buckingham Palace with the O.B.E. With 65 survivors of his ship, which was sunk by Italian torpedo-carrying 'planes when steaming to Malta, he was taken to Taborka, Tunisia, in November, 1941, exactly 12 months before the Allied landings in North Africa. For many months they were imprisoned in a lonely fort. Then, shortly before the Allied landings, Capt. Williams partly lost his hearing, and, through the American Consol, he was allowed to undergo special treatment in Tunisia. One night he awoke to find the Germans had arrived. His friend and himself spent three nights in a harem and others in shops, offices, and friendly Maltese homes. They masqueraded as natives, let their beards grow, wore ragged berets, and hunched their shoulders. Then a friend suggested that they should try to get to Le Kram, 12 miles away, but every crossing was guarded by sentries. By the influence of their friend, a coach belonging to

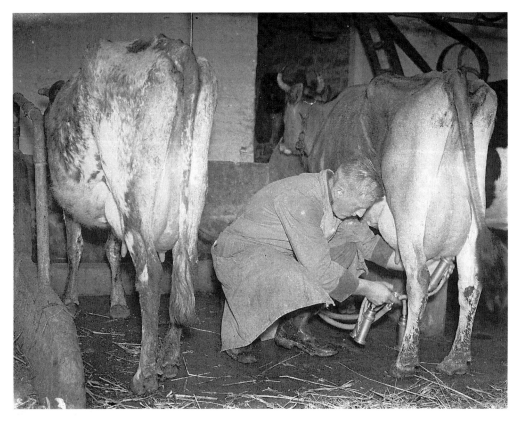

Minister of Agriculture's visit to Mr. Crowle's Coldharbour Farm, Bodmin, cows being milked. 6/1943

the Bey of Tunis was procured. It was a gaily-coloured affair. The chauffeur was in blue and the footman in a vivid costume. As they drove along they were suddenly halted. Their hearts stood still , but the natives apparently told the sentry that the Bey's coach must on no account be stopped, and they went on in grand style. Later they hid in a cemetery, dodged behind tombstones, and crouched in vaults till the danger of capture was over. That was the game of hide-and-seek they had to play till the great day came when the boys came marching in.   1/7/1943

Six Ancient Stones

While excavating at the rear of Solway's Garage, Marazanvose, recently, Mr. David Solway found six curious-looking stones about two feet below the ground, and sent them to the County Museum, Truro, for examination. Mr. G. Penrose expressed the opinion that the stones, known as "mummers" were used for pounding metallic ore or for grinding corn. They were in use from about 200 A.D. onwards for a considerable period. Around the stones, which seem to be of grey elvan, was a thick dark seam, which reference books on the subject say is sometimes the remains of a decayed body. This gives rise to the theory that the tools were buried with the body of their owner. Although they are sometimes found in other parts of the country, it is a rare occurrence to find several together in a pit.   8/7/1943

Independence Day Parade, Bodmin. United States soldiers passing by. *4/7/1943*

The Smallest School

Three pupils form the entire school at St. Agnes, Isles of Scilly, the smallest school in Britain. Under the guidance of their teacher, Miss E.B. Smith, they are enthusiastic salvage collectors, and have entered into competition with schools in the Penzance area. The population of St. Agnes is 50, and the scholars, aged 6, 8, and 11, cover several miles of territory in their quest for paper. 15/7/1943

Advertisement

CAN YOU KEEP A SECRET?

There's plenty of them in Britain now, and the Axis would dearly love to share them with you. Careless talk of any kind may give the enemy a clue and put him on his guard. Silence is more than golden – it's safe.

WHAT MUST I DO?

I don't discuss troop or ship movements with anyone.

I never talk about my war work or the position of factories or stores.

I don't write letters about bomb damage near me, or troops billeted on me, or friends getting embarkation leave.

If I've got a secret, I don't share it! Issued by the Ministry of Information. 22/7/1943

Advertisement

Salute The Home Guard

In Britain's darkest and finest hour they sprang to arms – that were not there! With shot gun, forgotten revolvers and sticks they watched the night sky: then the arms came, rifles, grenades, machine guns, and they learned to use them. After the day's work they

Bob Hope, American film star, entertaining the U.S. troops at Bodmin Barracks.

15/7/1943

Beach defences at Gyllyngvase beach, Falmouth, in the background. Sailors and locals enjoying the sun. *Summer 1943*

Salvage at Moorswater, (Liskard Rural District Council) council workers stacking bales of newspaper into a railway truck.   *31/7/1943*

drilled, practised, studied tactics – and now…an army, mighty to strike. On their day of rest they attack the power station, they defend the mill, they crawl, they patrol, they charge – Come on Jerry if you feel like it – But remember you will be welcomed on the beaches, at the cross-roads, at the street corner, everywhere in this island by the biggest, toughest citizen army in history! To-day, the Home Guard stands trained, armed, and equipped – another big job to which our savings have contributed. But the job's not finished yet. Victory demands more work – and more SAVINGS.

SAVE FOR VICTORY

Issued by the National Savings Committee   29/7/1943

Roman Milestone

Another link with the past, revealed by the ploughing up of new land, is a recent discovery at Mynheer Farm, near Gwennap Pit, which will undoubtedly throw fresh light on Cornwall during the Roman occupation of Cornwall. In 1941 Mr. Born and his son were ploughing a field on the highest part of the farm, when the plough struck a rock, which they dug up and put aside. Later the rains washed off the earth and exposed some lettering, which was noticed by Mr. Gerald Born, who comparing the inscription with that on the Roman milestone described in Daniel's *History of Cornwall*, decided that the stone must be saved. It is a granite stone, 3ft 7ins high, and 10ins wide, with a dressed face, 2ft 2ins by 7ins wide. Both Mr. Morton Nance and Mr. C. James (who is writing a history of Gwennap) agree that it is a roman milestone and date it 235-240 A.D. The inscription, which is in the usual abbreviated form, is here given approximately as it appears: 5/8/1943

IMP CAES ANT GOR DIA NO PIO FEL

In a letter published in the West Briton 19/8/1943 a translation is given as "To the Emperor Caesar Antonius Gordianus Happiness" or Fel may stand for Felici, agreeing with the other datives. It is believed that this Gordianus was Gordianus 111.

First War-Time Regatta

Point and Penpol Regatta, which is believed to be the only war-time regatta to be held in the county, was a great success on August Bank Holiday. The last regatta was held in 1939, and a large number of entries and many hundreds of spectators were present at its revival. To date, the proceeds for the Red Cross exceed £60.   5/8/1943

Cornwall War-Time Agricultural Executive Committee – Notice To Farmers

Schoolboy and schoolgirl Harvest Camps for students over 14 years of age are being organised throughout the County for the benefit of Farmers requiring help to gather the Harvest and for other work. *There then follows a list of the areas, Launceston, St. Germans, Wadebridge, Liskard, and Helston, with the name of the evacuated school and the number of boys or girls that the school would send.*   5/8/1943

Brickmaking Suggestions

A correspondent writes: "Considerable interest has been aroused in Gwennap area at the decision of Camborne-Redruth Urban Council to include the resuscitation of brick-making from clay at Pennance, Lanner, among suggestions forwarded to the Regional Controller of the Board of trade for the development of industry in the urban area after the war. The making of bricks from clay in about three acres of land on the south side of Carnmarth Hill and adjoining the main Redruth-Carharrack road was begun in the 60's of the last century, and the industry continued there for about 25 years. In its heyday it comprised four kilns, a moulding shed, drying shed and four chimneys, one of which was never used. The work had a siding on the old Redruth and Chacewater Railway, and many shipments of bricks were made from Devoran… Pennance bricks are to be found in many parts of the world. Forty years ago the writer saw in a building in Johannesburg bricks manufactured at Pennance".   12/8/1943

Relic Of Local Mint

The unearthing of a Cornish penny by Mr. T.C. Ducher, while working in a field at Chapel Farm, Tregajorran, Carn Brea, recalls an earlier period when there was a war-time shortage of copper. Of the inscription on the coin all that remains legible is "Dol-coath Mine". It has a crest which occupies the whole of one side and consists of a shield supported by two unicorns and surmounted by a baronial crown. The Latin inscription would doubtless read Pro Rege Et Populo, or For the King and the People. At about the time of the Napoleonic Wars permission was granted to certain concerns to coin token money. This was because of the shortage of State copper coins, a metal which was urgently needed to cover the bottoms of the ships-of-war. When these coins had served their purpose they were recalled, which would probably account for their now being comparatively rare.   26/8/1943

The crest was that of Lord de Dunstanville and the coin would have stated that it was "payable in cash notes at Dolcoath Mine", Camborne. It would have been issued in 1811 or 1812. All the Cornish Pennies were designed and manufactured by Thomas Halliday of Birmingham, they weighed approximately two-thirds of an ounce. Francis, Lord de Dunstanville and Basset, of Tehidy, is commemorated in the Monument on top of Carn Brea.

Mr. L. Roscorle of Lanreath, turnwrest ploughing at Liskeard Young Farmers Club Agricultural Demonstration. Turnwrest ploughs were also known as "up and over" ploughs.   *28/8/1943*

Horse Racing Again

Twenty-three year old Doxie, belonging to and ridden by Mr. W. Rail, of Budock, one of the best-known jumpers in Cornwall, was one of several well-known horses competing in a programme of jumping and of horse races seen by more than 2,000 people in St. Austell on Saturday. The meeting was organised by Mr. H. Cecil Rowse, of St. Austell, as a contribution to the Cornwall auctioneers' endeavour to raise £10,000 for the R.A.F. Pilots' and Air Crews Fund, known as the "Fund for the Few".   26/8/1943

Redruth Hospital Clinics

Owing to the call-up of medical officers, out-patients clinics at Camborne-Redruth Miners' and General Hospital, Redruth, are held as follows:
Medical – Mondays, 10.30 a.m., Mr. R.H.Blair; Thursdays, 2.30 p.m., Dr. L.W.Hale.
Surgical – Mondays, 2 p.m., Mr. G. O'Donnell; Thursdays, 10.30 a.m. Mr. T.M. Reid.
Gynaecology – Saturdays, 10 a.m., Dr. R. Pollock.
Dental – Saturdays, 10.30 a.m., Mr. W.H.C. Lean.
Gynaecology – Tuesdays, 2 p.m., Mr. J.G. Hastings Ince.
Ophthalmic – Wednesdays, 10.30 a.m., Mr. R.W. Payne.   2/9/1943

Women Of 47

Women born in 1896 are to register on Saturday, September 11th.   2/9/1943

Advertisment

Truro Garages, Ltd., Truro   'phone 2353

Pneumatic Tyres for Fordson tractors are practically unobtainable, but our new Road Band, fitted in seven minutes, can now be purchased. Limited quantity only available for the time being.   2/9/1943

Bathing Warning

Before the war a red flag was flown from a pole on the car park at Perranporth to warn people when bathing was dangerous. The recent bathing fatality at Perranporth has brought out the fact that the flag is no longer flown owing to war conditions.
A holiday maker from London who was a Czechoslovakian refugee, was carried out to sea when bathing at Perranporth at low tide. There was a terrific undercurrent with high waves. His body was subsequently recovered.   9/9/1943

Best News Yet

Britain received with jubilation, last night, the best news of the war; the news of Italy's surrender.   9/9/1943

Cornishmen Calling

Cornishmen at home and in America will hear the story of the Duchy and its people in "Transatlantic Call; People to People", next Sunday, on the B.B.C. Forces wavelength. Capt. Donald Dickson, dockmaster at a Cornish port, will tell listeners of the changes in the harbour where he has watched shipping for 17 years; the Helston Furry Dance will be described by 70-year-old Peter Sandry, several members of whose family are in the U.S.A. Sidney Hodge, who has managed it since 1910, will tell stories of the Duchy Oyster Farm. Bob Lovelock, a tin miner and Charlotte Dunn, who works on camouflage nets, are among other broadcasters. A male voice choir of police and Civil Defence workers, conducted by the Rev. C. Daly Atkinson, will sing Cornish folk songs. The narrator will be Bernard Fishwick, the well-known Cornish broadcaster now serving in the Army.   23/9/1943

Russia's War Horses

A tribute to the part war horses are playing in the magnificent successes of the Russian Armies was paid be Major Maurice Petherick, M.P., when he opened Mylor and District horse, comic dog show, and sports, at Canera Frm, Mylor, on Saturday, in aid of the R.S.P.C.A. Fund for Russian War Horses. The effort realised over £100. Mr. R.J. Rogers, who introduced Major Petherick, explained that Mrs. F.P. Stephens was the originator of the idea of holding the show. The cavalry horses on the Russian front were doing a remarkable job. Many were killed and others badly wounded. This meant taking them back to sick bays or hospitals, and he urged those present to give all they could to help provide veterinary treatment. 23/9/1943

Cornwall's Oldest Resident

Cornwall's oldest resident, Mrs. Elizabeth Uren, who was within three months of her 105th birthday, died yesterday at Treveale Farm, Zennor, the residence of her nephew and niece, Mr. and Mrs. E.H. Loosemore, with whom she had lived for more than 30 years. Mrs. Uren was born at Zennor on January 15th, 1839, her parents being Mr. and Mrs. Hollow, Trendrine Farm, who lived to be 99 and 96 years of age respectively. Mrs. Uren was one of a family of 15 children, and she had spent the greater part of her life at Zennor. At one time she was at Penzance, where she married, and later carried on a general stores and shop in Causewayhead, her husband died many years ago, and she had no children. Until she was more than 102 years of age, Mrs. Uren was able to come downstairs, and she retained her faculties until about two days before her death. When past her 103rd birthday, she was able to sit up in bed knitting and sewing, making socks as well as doing work on a patchwork quilt. She took a keen interest in the news of the war, and was not a bit scared of aeroplanes she could hear overhead. Mrs. Uren had a hearty appetite, and ate ordinary meals after she had celebrated her 103rd birthday, and it was her custom to have half a pasty and a bottle of stout at night, the other piece of pasty and some more stout or a glass of wine being reserved for her to consume during the night. 14/10/1943

Advertisement

For Sale

Firewood (Logs), lorry load, 50s; half load, 25s. sacks, 2s 6d.; free delivery to 10 miles radius. P.A.M. Ltd., 15, St. Clements-st., Truro. 14/10/1943

On Way To Rome

Vincent Curnow, a secondary school boy, of Thomas-street, Porthleven, has had a reply to a letter which he wrote to General Montgomery, Commander of the Eight Army. "Thank you so much for your letter and good wishes", the General writes. "We are now well on our way to Rome. Next it will be Berlin. Thank you also for your kind offer of tea and Cornish Cream. I hope I shall be able to accept it in the near future". 21/10/1943

Nobody Available

The position relating to the suspension of Malpas Ferry services was explained to a meeting of Cornwall Highways Committee, at Bodmin, on Friday. The Clerk (Mr. L.P. New) stated that in January the headmistress of St. Michael Penkevil School wrote drawing attention to the difficulties she and others were experiencing through the cessation of the ferry services at Malpas. The ferry, operated by a rowing boat, was a public one, the franchise being vested in Lord Falmouth. The matter had been taken up with Lord

Falmouth's agent, with a view to the services being resumed, but Lord Falmouth's agent replied that they were unable to get anyone to run the ferry. 21/10/1943

Ship's M.O. At 76
Although he had retired from practice there, Dr. J. Welby Haughton, of Falmouth, volunteered at the age of 73, to serve as a medical officer in an ocean-going steamship in August, 1940. He has since travelled thousands of miles, and his ship was three times attacked by Italian bombers in the Mediterranean. In about two months he hopes to rejoin his ship, which is being refitted. At one time Dr. Haughton practised in Truro. 28/10/1943

Americans Welcomed
Officers and men of the American Forces were entertained by the mayor and Corporation of a South-West town on Friday. At a dinner to the officers the mayor said as that was probably his last function in that office he considered himself very fortunate in having the honour of welcoming the Americans and an opportunity of proposing the toast of President Roosevelt. "We have as much respect and confidence in him as in Mr. Churchill", said the Mayor, "and we are sure that the peace problems will be justly handled if he has the necessary support". 28/10/1943

A Famous Sire
At a Guernsey sale at Reading, on Tuesday, Mr. G. Blight, of Tregonning, Breage, bought for 80 guineas a bull calf by the Guernsey bull which made the record price of 3,400 guineas. At the same sale Mr. Blight sold eight heifers at an average of £202 2s 6d each. 28/10/1943

Truro Home Guard river patrol boat "Mistral". *30/10/1943*

Home Again – Cornish Prisoners Of War Return

"There is no doubt that the Germans are cracking. You can tell that from the way they behave and from the way they are fed and clothed. They have a dreadful fear that the Russians will reach them before the British do". This is what Mr. William Williams, 6, Sandow's-lane, St. Ives, told a *West Briton* correspondent, on Friday, when he returned to his home after having been a prisoner of war for over three years. Like his many companions on the mercy ships, Mr. Williams was full of praise for the Red Cross, saying that without that organisation the prisoners would not have existed.

Mr. Williams, Mr. C .Coad and Mr.P. Care, who were all members of the St. Ives Ambulance before the war, had been taken prisoners when France collapsed.   4/11/1943

Capt. G.T. Williams Escapes

Capt. G.T. Williams, only son of the late Capt. Gage Williams, of Scorrier House, who has been a prisoner of war in Italy, has escaped. After having walked over 300 miles in enemy occupied territory, in 33 days, and living mostly on grapes, he managed to get through to our lines.   4/11/1943

Old 'Uns Pleased

Many of the older farmers and farm hands, who swear by a horse and disclaim the virtues of "them there mechanical contraptions", were delighted at Probus Young Farmers' Club ploughing match, on Saturday, when the horse beat the tractor. The ploughing match and hedging competition were held on the farm of Mr. E. Kendall, of Golden Manor. A special prize was offered for the best work done by any member of the club. The judges had a difficult job, as the competitors were entered in different classes. Three did tractor work, one commercial horse ploughing, and one best horse ploughing. The judges awarded the prize to Norman Bilkey, of Gargus, Tregoney, who used a single-furrow turnwrest plough.   4/11/1943

Land Army Fund

Nearly 1,500 members of the Women's Land Army are employed in Cornwall, and to date just over £170 has been raised in the county for the organisation's Benevolent fund. The fund was formed just over a year ago with the approval of the Ministry of Agriculture and Fisheries, and it has two main objects. The first is to help cases of illness and hardship among members of the Land Army now which are not adequately covered by existing State schemes – for instance, when a patient leaves hospital, long convalescence and massage or electrical treatment are often needed, for which the 12s or 15s per week received from insurance is inadequate. Second, the fund intend to help Land Army volunteers when the time comes for them to return to peace-time occupations. For these purposes it is estimated that at least £100,000 will be required. Over £36,000 has so far been raised, of which £10,000 was a grant from H.M. Treasury.   11/11/1943

Lost And Found

Lost, in Redruth, Sunday last, wallet, containing treasury notes, identity card, clothing coupons, and important documents – Reward on returning to 26, Trefusis-road, Redruth or Police Station.   11/11/1943

"Q" Is 80

The greatest living Cornishman will celebrate his 80th birthday on Sunday, for it was on November 21st, 1863, that Arthur Thomas Quiller-Couch was born at Bodmin, eldest son of Dr. Thomas Quiller-Couch and a grandson of the famous ichthyologist, Jonathan Couch, of Polperro. Sir Arthur's many friends and admirers are delighted that on the eve of his 80th birthday he is remarkably well and vigorous, and that during the summer he has been rowing as usual in the familiar red boat, the Picotee, with Lady Quiller-Couch and their daughter, Miss Foy Quiller-Couch. 18/11/1943

'Bus Top Strikes Bridge

The top of a large double-decker Western National Omnibus struck the low overhead bridge carrying the main Great Western line over Bond-street, Redruth, on Thursday. The vehicle, which was carrying a good many passengers, was bound for Falmouth, and instead of proceeding down Station-hill, in the usual way, and up Falmouth-road, the driver, Mr. Phillips, of Camborne, turned from Station-road into Bond-street, where the bridge is not sufficiently high to permit a double-decker 'bus to pass underneath it. There was a some-what violent collision with the bridge, which resulted in the roof of the 'bus being smashed and glass broken. Passengers were shaken by the sudden stopping of the vehicle, the roof of which had become tightly embedded in the ironwork of the bridge, but only two sustained slight injuries. It was some time before the bus could be released from the bridge and traffic had to be diverted. 25/11/1943
This bridge is 12ft 3ins high and replaced a wooden one at the end of the 19th century. Buses and lorries continued to become stuck under the bridge.

Cycle Thefts: Hard Labour

"Cycle stealing is getting far too prevalent, and it is the duty of the Bench to support the Police trying to stamp out this sort of thing", said the Chairman (Mr. W. Chappell) at Falmouth Police Court, on Monday, announcing the Bench's decision that William Frank Rothman, aged 37, a naval stoker, and a native of Paddington, should be sent to prison for three months hard labour. *He pleaded guilty to having stolen two bicycles, but only sold one. He asked for another theft of a cycle and the theft of a watch, both of which he had sold, to be taken into account. He was a deserter and had been in prison before.* 25/11/1943

Correspondence: Redruth Cattle Market

Sir – Those covered-in shelters in the Cattle Market at Redruth, were they erected for the purpose of protecting motor cars, leaving the cattle – as at present – in pens in the open, exposed to all weathers? I ask you. Yours faithfully, F.A. Fraser, Major. 25/11/1943

Motor Cars etc. For Sale

Let The Morrison Electric Vehicle solve your transport problems. Large numbers of these vehicles are in operation throughout the British Isles, and are giving first-class service. Can we send you details? H.T.P. Motors Ltd., Princes Garage, Truro. 'phone 2581.
25/11/1943

Diphtheria At Hayle

The Public Health Committee submitted to West Penwith Rural Council, on Thursday, a report from Dr. R.H. Hadfield (medical officer of health) stating that ten cases of diphtheria had been notified, seven occurring at Hayle in four separate families, and three in one family at Madron. All the cases were removed to the County Isolation Hospital at Truro, together with several contacts who were discovered to be virulent carriers although not suffering from the disease. 2/12/1943

Lostwithiel Mincemeat Problems

The Chairman thought the fat allocation for the town ought to be increased seeing that they had no British Restaurant or pasty scheme… It was decided to apply to the Ministry for an increased fat allocation. Mrs. F. Harvey said it was unfair that at whist drives people were able to get so much food for refreshments. It meant that the food was taken from the public supply… Mr. Robins asked if the food officer could advise him how he could divide up 96 lbs of mincemeat with 1,751 registrations.   9/12/1943

Water And Light For Country-Dwellers

Urging the provision of water and electricity supplies for dwellers in rural areas, Mrs. Beatrice Wright, M.P. for the Bodmin Division, in the debate on an amendment to the Address in the House of Commons, on Tuesday, said that the Inland Water Survey had yet to turn its attention to Cornwall. In this county alone there were 97 out of the 177 parishes without a piped water supply. The rural water supply situation was becoming more acute – consumption rising and yet rain-water tanks were still the recognised water supply in many villages, and in many farms the only supply was from stagnant ponds. The whole problem, she thought, could be greatly alleviated by the supply of electricity. How much more economical to carry wires than pipes many miles, and the farm would have the added benefit of electricity for pumping, lighting, heating and cooking. While the House discussed and set up committees, the woman in her constituency carried heavy buckets to and fro, up hill and down dale, cooked on archaic grates in dingy dark rooms lit by kerosene lamps, while springs were bubbling, streams running, and the grid marched through the county.   9/12/1943

Advertisement

Waiting For Houses – 200 To 300 People At Falmouth

… Ald. Harris said the Town Planning and Building Committee were very wise in preparing for post-war housing, but houses would cost double what they paid for building in pre-war days and the tenants would not be able to pay an economical rent. Unless the Government came forward with subsidies or grants, it would be a serious matter for the finances of the town, and it would not be fair that the ratepayers who were not council tenants should be called upon to find the difference.   16/12/1943

Advertisement

War–time standard models, complete with pump and tools, from the B.S.A. Dealer in your district. £8 19s 5d including Purchase Tax. 20/12/1943

Plague of Rats – Newquay Call To Combat Menace
The awful destruction being done by rats was mentioned by the Chairman, Mr. E.T. Luke, at Newquay Urban Council, on Tuesday. He emphasised that householders as well as farmers should assist the authorities in dealing with the menace. Each and everyone must do his level best in the matter, and so remove the pest which was disastrous to the country. Mr. H. Hocking said he had never known so many rats in the fields and hedges. It was left to the clerk and sanitary inspector to take steps to comply with the Infestation Order, 1943. 23/12/1943

Sewage As Fertiliser
The profitable disposal of sewage as a fertiliser was discussed by the Executive Committee of the Cornwall branch of the Council for the Preservation of Rural England, at Truro, on Tuesday. Mr. F.V. Rolfe reported that Mr.W.E. Arnold-Foster was now in touch with a noted scientist who had taken him to see the works at Kingston-upon-Thames, where a process was being applied to sewage that rendered it profitable as fertiliser… Mr. R. Bennett Webb said that he was very interested in the matter, as Truro would find such a method of profitable disposal of sewage most helpful. 23/12/1943

Advertisement

**While Shepherds Watch…Carn Brea calls to Cornishmen
And Women at Home, in the Forces and Overseas**

It costs **ONE SHILLING** every minute to maintain the Camborne-Redruth Miners' and General Hospital (the only Centre in Cornwall containing Specialist Services for the treatment of Cancer, Abnormal Maternity and Women's Diseases), and every hour valuable lives are being saved. For how long will you help us to carry on – how many lives will you help us to save? Write your Christmas prescription now, please, and send it to the President, at the Appeal Office, Smith's Buildings, Alma Place, Redruth. So that others may live. Telephone: Redruth 25

Cheques, etc., should be made payable to "Viscount Clifton", and crossed "Hospital Fund Account". 23/12/1943

The National Health Service did not start until 1948 and the hospitals were funded before then by subscription, many firms and individuals paying into local insurance schemes, or by the Public Assistance Board for those who could not pay. The Beveridge Report advocated the bringing in of the free National Health Service. The above hospital was opened in 1863 as the West Cornwall Hospital for Convalescent Miners, over the years other departments were opened. It was closed in 1996 when the services it offered were transferred to Treliske Hospital in Truro.

Quiet Christmas In Cornwall
Although they were unable to celebrate their fifth war-time Christmas with all the rich Usage's and the reunions associated with the great festival, the majority of Cornish people achieved something of the traditional merriment, and tremendous efforts were made to provide the children with toys, good fare, and parties which are the just due of childhood. Even food rationing was made to yield advantage by clever housewives, who had planned for months to make the festive menu a delightful and surprising contrast with everyday fare. 30/12/1943

1944

Sea Fisheries Control – Terms Of Draft Convention

The draft convention drawn up at the International Fisheries Conference held in London, in October, was published on Thursday. Minimum sizes are specified for 10 varieties of fish. Expressed in inches, (the draft convention used centimetres), they are:- Soles, 8·26, plaice, witches, lemon soles and megrims, 9.05; cod and haddock, 9.44, turbot and brill, 9·84, and hake, 11·81. Fish caught in the waters covered by the convention, which from the tip of the snout to the extreme end of the tail fin are below these lengths must be returned to the sea.   3/1/1944

Brighter Homes In 1944

Thanks to Africa we are to have a brighter Britain. From January 1st, manufacturers of furniture polish will be able to increase their output as a special drive by Tanganyika producers, which has resulted in greater supplies of beeswax being made available. This will not make the total amount of floor and furniture polish available more than one-half of pre-war output, but it will be sufficient to ensure that the housewife will be able to remove a little austerity dullness from her home. Output of boot and shoe polishes will also be increased.   3/1/1944

Rat Destruction

The destruction of rats was referred to at a meeting of St. Austell Rural Council, on Friday, by the Vice-Chairman, (Mr. F. James) who said the County War Agricultural Committee had records of 80,000 rats destroyed in the last 15 months, and 33,000 in the last five months, and there were great banks of them still untouched. The figures took no account of the tremendous number poisoned which the committee's officers did not see. Rabbit trappers said they had never seen so many rats as they had seen this year.   6/1/1944

Misuse Of Petrol

Vigilance of two special constables led to the conviction at Camborne, on Tuesday, of Fred Richards, Horsedowns, Crowan, for the use of petrol for an unauthorised purpose. Inspector G.Warne said defendant was seen by Constables Williams and May to motor to Praze and there drop a young lady. Asked why he was using the car, defendant, who had driven off in the direction of Helston, stated that he was proceeding to work at Camborne, but was returning home for his lunch bag. He was subsequently seen driving in the direction of Camborne, but he did not put in an appearance at his place of employment, and was not expected to do so. The prosecution submitted that defendant used his car solely to take a young lady home to Praze, and that his subsequent journey in the direction of Camborne was an unsuccessful attempt to "blind" the police. Defendant, who wrote pleading guilt, was fined £2 and 10s. costs.   6/1/1944

So Falmouth Arose – From The Ashes Of Arwenack House

Falmouth is unique among the boroughs of Britain in that it can show the actual home of its founder within the borough boundaries. Down to Tudor times the harbour of Falmouth was in the mayoralty of Truro, and where the town of Falmouth now stands was the estate of Arwenack, the home of the Killigrew family. In the 16th century the Arwenack Manor House is stated to have been the finest and most costly house in the county, containing numerous and highly-decorated rooms. "The owner, John Killigrew, with John Treffry of Fowey, was the builder of Pendennis Castle. The proximity of the manor house to the castle was its undoing, for in the Civil War it was set on fire in order that it should not be occupied by the Parliamentary forces. In the time of James 1st, Sir John Killigrew obtained permission to build four houses, and had made further plans to develop the property, including plans for a quay and custom-house. He met with opposition from Penryn and Truro, but the Civil war intervening, the growth of a town was stopped. After the Restoration, Sir Peter Killigrew reaped the reward of his loyalty to the Stuart cause in the shape of a charter of incorporation for a town to be called Falmouth. This was in August 1660. From that date the future of the new town was assured, but Arwenack House was not rebuilt, though the remains were made habitable and are still used as a dwelling-house. A very scarce old print… shows its appearance in 1786. 6/1/1944

Two Books Each – Needed For City's 25,000 Target
If each of the citizens of Truro gives two books, the success of the city's book drive, which began on Saturday, is assured… The books are needed for the entertainment and relaxation of the Forces, who, without question, deserve whatever enjoyment civilians can provide for them; for restocking bombed libraries, in which 8,000,000 volumes have been destroyed, and also for re-pulping for munitions. 10/1/1944

Claimed By Germans – Convoy Attacked Off Cornish Coast
A "major success" by German motor torpedo boats against a convoy off the Cornish coast early on Thursday morning was claimed by the German News Agency on Thursday." They sank without loss to themselves, five ships, totalling 12,500 tons, and one escort vessel.", the Agency said. The M.T.B's broke off the engagement only after the last torpedo had been fired, and returned to base without damage, it added. 10/1/1944

Empty Toothpaste Tubes
By placing empty toothpaste, shaving cream, and metal tubes generally in special collecting boxes on the chemists' counter, the salvage-minded citizen can directly assist British prisoners-of-war. For the valuable metals obtained from 230 of these tubes when sold for munition-making, will provide enough money to send out a Red Cross prisoner of war parcel. 10/1/1944

Girls Of 18 Must Register
All women born between July 1st, 1925, and December 31st, 1925, both dates inclusive, are required to register at a local office of the Ministry of Labour and national Service on Saturday next. Those already rendering whole-time paid service in the W.A.A.F., WR.E.N.S. or nursing and medical services attached to these Forces, or who are registered under the ex-cotton operatives registration, are not required to register. 10/1/1944

Advertisement
5lbs. of coal saved in one day by 40,000 homes will provide enough fuel to build a Churchill tank. Is YOUR home saving fuel to make Churchill tanks?
Save Fuel For Battle. 13/1/1944

Awarded B.E.M.
Mr. John Curnow, of 30, Chariot-road, Illogan Highway, has been awarded the British Empire Medal. He has been employed as a miner at East Pool and Agar Mine since 1900

and is a member of the Fire Guard at Illogan. 13/1/1944

Advertisement
Did you forget this? From time to time the Government issues warnings against the dangers of diphtheria. Of every 50 cases of diphtheria, two or three die. Immunisation protects against these dangers. If your child has not been immunised, see that this is done now. Issued by the Ministry of Information. 13/1/1944

Lighting Fires Without Paper
Most people are anxious to observe the order that makes it an offence to burn clean paper, but are wondering how they are to manage if they have fires to light every day, have no stocks of paper, and take only one newspaper a day. "Surely," they argue, "we can use newspapers? A fire can't be lit without paper!" The answer is that it can. Here is the "recipe". Clear the grate, keeping cinders to use again, and only throwing away ash. Take a short stick of wood and shave all four sides to within an inch of the end, using a sharp penknife and not breaking the shavings off. Your piece of wood now looks like a brush or whisk. Place the shaved stick upright in the grate, shavings downwards (they curve outwards so that the stick will keep upright). Arrange more pieces of wood around this centre stick to form a pyramid and add a few small pieces of coal. Light the shavings at the bottom of the stick. When well alight, add more coal and cinders. 17/1/1944

"Monty"
Mr. R.Rowe, an old "Contemptible" of the last war, and Mrs. Rowe, Basset-road, Treleigh, who wrote conveying Christmas greetings to General B.N. Montgomery and informing him that they had decided to name their baby Montgomery, have received a letter of thanks from the General, who added: "I am honoured that you should call your son after me. Good luck to him." The letter is being preserved as a treasured possession. 20/1/1944

Advertisement
In the districts where you can get it – make do with one slice of Ryvita with each meal. We must share it round very carefully. 20/1/1944

Brothers On Leave
Three Truro brothers who have been home on leave after serving together since the beginning of the war, first in France and then with the Eighth Army throughout the North Africa campaign, including the siege of Torbruk. They are Newman, Frederick and Leslie Baker, of 19, Edward-street, Truro. 20/1/1944

300 Guineas For Bull
At the recent Guernsey sale at Reading, Mr. George Blight, of Tregonning, Breage, bought for 300 guineas for his Tregonning and Trelowarren herds, the most beautifully bred yearling bull Rogerum, whose sire is brother to the 3,400 guinea bull sold on October 28th, 1943. This is probably the highest price ever paid for a Guernsey bull for Cornwall.
20/1/1944

Save The Peel
Oranges will seen in the shops in the near future. Scarcity has taught us to value them as they should be valued and to use the peel as well as the pulp. To skin orange easily, dip them in and out of boiling water. Make candied peel with the skins. 24/1/1944

Newquay Book Salvage Drive at the Girls County School, Newquay. *31/1/1944*

Used Same Ticket Twice

Corpl. Allen Arthur Furze, R.A.F. pleaded guilty at Newquay, on Tuesday, to travelling on the G.W.R. without paying the fare. The prosecution's case was that on December 8th defendant was travelling from Newquay to Plymouth, and he handed the inspector a ticket on which he noticed the date had been interfered with. Defendant said he had used the other half. He used the return portion before the forward portion as he had a lift on a lorry. He offered to pay the fare, which was not accepted. When interviewed by a railway detective, defendant admitted that he did it as he was short of money. He said he had used the forward half to Plymouth, but it was not collected and he used it again. He erased the date, borrowed a rubber stamp and put another date on. The amount of the Forces' fare was 4s.4p. – Defendant was dealt with under the Probation of Offenders Act, and the case was dismissed on payment of 15s. expenses, 4s. costs, and the 4s.4d. unpaid fare. *27/1/1944*

Instant Death – Young Miner's Fall At South Crofty

The action of a young miner in venturing into part of the underground workings at South Crofty where, it was stated, he had no right to be for the purpose for which he went there, was related to Mr. Barrie B. Bennetts (county coroner) at an inquest at Pool, on Thursday, on Douglas Henry Couch, aged 19, Pondsbridge-hill, Liskeard. Couch was killed through falling through a disused stope – Mr. J.V. Ratcliffe represented the mining company and Mr. R. Butler (H.M. Inspector of Mines) also attended... The Coroner, who sat without a jury, returned a verdict of "Accidental death", observing that to have caused such a regrettable accident deceased must have been doing what he ought not to have done.   31/1/1944

Sizes At A Glance

The clear marking, in inches, of the sizes of women's and maids' underwear and night wear is provided for in an Order just issued by the Board of Trade. The regulation, which has been introduced in order to avoid confusion on the part of the customer when making her purchase and so preventing a possible wastage of coupons, will apply to both utility and non-utility garments, and will come into operation on March 1st. The same order lays down new specifications for these garments designed to secure improved production and fitting and better coupon value. In many cases, for example, more cloth may be used to prevent the manufacture of skimped garments.   31/1/1944

Newspapers As Tablecloths

The suggestion of a Board of Trade official that to ease pressure on the laundries, people should eat their meals on bare boards or newspapers has not been enthusiastically received by Cornish launderers. An officer of the Cornish branch of the Institution of British Launderers commented that the suggestion was the most utter rot he had ever read. There is a shortage of labour, but that had been offset to a large extent by making deliveries only once a fortnight, by preventing, by mutual agreement, the overlapping of laundry areas, and by cutting out calls on customers off the main route of the laundry vans. The machinery used for table linen and sheets can only be used for such flat work and cannot be turned over to meeting the needs of the Armed Forces.   3/2/1944

Wasted Hours – Farmers And Double Summertime

"One hour summertime is bad enough for agriculture – let alone two", declared Mr. J.H. Sloman, senior vice-chairman, at the annual meeting of Truro branch of Cornwall Farmers Union, at Truro , yesterday. – The Chairman (Mr. P.O. Eddy) presided. Double summertime, Mr. Sloman said, was causing the farmers a lot of anxiety and unnecessary trouble. During the last two months they had scarcely known what to do with their men for the first 1½ hours in the mornings, and in the months to come the men would be leaving work at the time they were most busy. The men were on the farm too many hours before they started work, and then to ask them to continue, even at overtime, after 10 or 12 hours seemed unreasonable. They were looking forward to the time when this would be put right.   3/2/1944

Women's Land Army Wants 5,000 Milkmaids

The Women's Land Army, which re-opened recruiting recently, wants 5,000 more volunteers between 17 and 35 years of age, during the next few months, for key jobs. Lady Denman, director of the W.L.A. said in London yesterday, that 5,000 were needed for milking alone. Other key jobs were general farming, tractor driving, and rat destruction. Volunteers must be intelligent, strong and able to take responsibility. They must be prepared to work. The minimum cash wage was 22s 6d for a 48-hour week in winter, and a 50-hour week in summer. Milkers could earn from £4 to £5 a week with overtime, but too much overtime is not encouraged, as the work is hard.

Boys and girls between 14 and 19, who, with official approval, undertake seasonal work in agriculture from camps, are to have their minimum rate of pay increased from 8d to 9d per hour, by decision of the Agricultural Board yesterday.   3/2/1944

Flowers And Coupons

The Post office at St. Mary's, Isles of Scilly, declined on and from Tuesday, (February 1st) to accept any further packages of flowers unless accompanied by the appropriate coupons issued by the War Agricultural Committee. It is understood the committee will grant an individual gift coupon should he wish to send a few flowers to a friend. Throughout the season coupons have had to accompany packages of flowers consigned by the steamboat, and the system has worked very well. The Soleil d'Or season is practically finished, and the cup varieties such as Spur, Ervine, Berkley and King Alfred are now starting to bloom. Some of the most advanced cup flowers were damaged by stormy weather, but luckily the cup season is not as yet in full swing.

Growers are rapidly coming to the end of their coupons. There are a few broccoli about but not sufficient for export to the mainland.   3/2/1944

Tom Reece At Camborne

The Camborne Literary Institute was crowded on Saturday for the visit of Tom Reece, well-known English professional billiards player, who played exhibition games of billiards and snooker with members of the institute, and also gave a display of fancy strokes… Reece said that during the past 2½ years he had been responsible for raising over £10,000 for the Red Cross Sportsmen's Section through his exhibitions up and down the country.   10/2/1944

Advertisement

Ophelia Snodkins loved to ride *on her bicycle*
On the crown of the road instead of the side.
No signal she gave as she swerved to the right
So a sprightly young life met its end that night.
Let Ophelia's ghost be a warning to you
If you wish to live to a hundred and two.
　　LOOK OUT IN THE BLACK-OUT
The Western National   10/2/1944

Plaice By 'Plane

As a large aeroplane passed over the a town in the South West of England on Friday evening, two ladies sitting by their fireside heard a thud on the window. On going outside to investigate they saw by the light of a torch a large plaice all cleaned and ready for the table. The impress of the fish could plainly be seen on the window, but the glass remained unbroken because the fish hit the cross-frame of the window. Did the airmen lose their supper? The ladies enjoyed their breakfast next morning.   10/2/1944

From Bank To Mine

The first "Bevan Boy" to be called from Truro for the mines is Mr. Alfred Benney, 80, Kenwyn-street, Truro, son of Mr. and Mrs. J. Benney. He left on Monday for Monmouthshire. Previous to his call-up, he was a clerk at Lloyds Bank, Falmouth.   10/2/1944

Cinema Appeals

At the Palace Theatre, Perranporth, each evening last week a repatriated prisoner of war, Mr. Wood, was introduced to the audience by Miss M.A. Smith (assistant commandant of the Perranporth Red Cross Detachment). A film of the repatriation of prisoners of war was shown, and Mr. Wood spoke of the work of the Red Cross in sending parcels to the prisoners in enemy hands, how they were eagerly looked for ward to and without them they were all very short of food.   10/2/1944

Youngest D.S.O.

Lieut. Peter Haydon, of Heamoor, Penzance, who was awarded the D.S.O. for conspicuous conduct at the Salerno landings. Aged 20, he is the youngest D.S.O. in the British Army.
                                                                                      17/2/1944

Advertisement

Where would you and I be?
Harry was a gardener
Tommy was a baker
While Robert worked in one of those big Banks.
Now – Harry's in the infantry,
And Tom's behind a gun,
And when Robert volunteered he joined the Tanks.

Now where would you and I be
Without Bob and Tom and Harry?
We owe them so much more than just our thanks –
For Harry fights in Italy,
And Tom's downed twenty Huns,
And Robert's got a medal in the Tanks!
Salute the Soldier!   17/2/1944

Flower Ban Flouted

Saying that he was given a few flowers to take back to the hospital and nursing home at Penzance, a taxicab owner tried to board the local mail steamer at St. Mary's, Isles of Scilly, on Wednesday, with 290 bunches. On Thursday he was fined a total of £10 by The Isles of Scilly magistrates.   17/2/1944

Medicine To Him

William Richard Glasson, of 60, Trevean-road, Penzance, was charged at Penzance Police Court, on Monday, with buying a pint of beer for James Nicholls, of Boswarthen Madron, who is a youth under 18. Nicholls was summoned for aiding and abetting the offences – Frank Nicholls, the father, who had earlier been fined 2s 6d for allowing a mule to stray, told the Bench he did not agree with his son being on licensed premises, but added "Beer is medicine to him: he has been drinking it since he was two or three years old. He was weak when he was younger." – When Supt. F.G. Beale pointed out that it was an offence to give a child under seven intoxicating liquor except as a medicine, the father said the beer had been given as medicine, it was given in a spoon for his appetite – Nicholls was fined £1 and Glasson 10s.   17/2/1944

St Day Fatality

A fatal accident occurred on Wednesday afternoon at the bottom of Church-hill, which abuts on the main St. Day to Carharrack road. A young Canadian dispatch rider was involved in a head-on crash with a U.S. Army truck, driven by a coloured member of the U.S. Forces.   24/2/1944

Giant Whale – Washed Up On St. Agnes

A whale, 66 feet long, probably one of the largest ever seen on the shores of Southern England has been washed up on the beach at St. Agnes. The whale was first seen early on Thursday morning by a coastguard patrol. It was floating on the sea, and in the moonlight he thought it was a bomber forced down. Later in the day the whale, which is of the Rorqual or Whalebone family, was high and dry on the rocks, and a source of interest to evacuated children and villagers.   24/2/1944

Doors Open To Women

Falmouth Chamber of Commerce has decided to elect women , who are responsible for the conduct of businesses, as members of the chamber. May years ago when the subject was introduced there was a general feeling against opening the chamber to women. It is now felt that women, in many cases conducting businesses in the absence of their husbands away serving and those who are widows engaged in trading, will be of value to the organisation.   24/2/1944

Dog Show Gift

As a result of their Boxing Day effort, Truro and District Canine Society have, this week, sent a cheque for 100 guineas to the Duke of Gloucester's Red Cross and St. John Fund. This result is all the more commendable when it is taken into account that the entries

Pendowrie Hostel near Upton Cross, Liskeard. Hilary Webster, aged 6, from Tottenham, receiving an American Red Cross parcel from the Matron, Mrs. Wiseman.   *25/2/1944*

Rat Catching at Liskeard. Mr. R. Crabb with Joan Moore and Mary Morley. 1/3/1943

were confined to a radius of 25 miles, and it is an indication of the great enthusiasm on the part of the workers. 2/3/1944

More Wheat In Bread

By the beginning of April the British public will be getting an almost pure wheat loaf again. Mr. C.A. Loombe, Director of Cereal Products, for the Food Ministry, said that oats, barley, and rye had formed 10 per cent of flour. The use of oats and barley had been stopped. By the beginning of next month we shall have only 2½ per cent of rye and 97½ per cent of wheat in our flour and bread. Alone among the countries of Europe the United Kingdom is enjoying unrationed flour and bread. 6/3/1944

Three Mile Limit

A promise to take steps to see if some arrangement could be arrived at whereby large foreign vessels fishing out of Newlyn were made to keep outside the three-mile limit, was given by Mr. Alec Beechman, M.P., on Saturday, when he spoke at a largely attended meeting of the Mount's Bay Fishermen's Association, at Newlyn. Mr. E.T. Vingoe, who presided, said the breaking of the three-mile restriction was being winked at by the authorities, and as a result the inshore fishing grounds were being destroyed and their livelihood taken away. If there was a big influx of trawl fish as a result, pilchards would not be wanted and they might as well destroy their nets. He was afraid that the Fishery Board were not interested in inshore fishermen. They were small business men, working their own craft, whose sons were fighting for their country, and maintained that they had a perfect right to safeguard their livelihood.   9/3/1944

Cornwall's First Motorist

The passing of Mr. George Herbert Powell, at his residence, Glan Mor, Falmouth-road, Truro, on Tuesday, recalls the advent of the first motor car in Cornwall, about 44 years ago. A dentist by profession, Mr. Powell, when a young man took an immense interest in motor cars, and was proud of the distinction of being the first owner of a motor car in the county. Older Truronians will remember the excitement created by the appearance of Mr. Powell's car in the streets of the city about 1900. Mr. Powell was fond of relating his experience on the first trip of any distance, to Perranporth, when on the homeward journey engine trouble developed and the vehicle was pushed several miles back to the city. Mr. Powell's interest in automobiles never diminished and he was always to the fore in changing over to new models.   9/3/1944

Killed By Bomb

Service honours were accorded at the funeral of Miss Doris Williams, aged 22, daughter of Mr. and Mrs. Cecil Williams, formerly of Constantine. Miss Williams, who lived with her parents, was returning home, when a bomb exploded near her and she was killed outright. Her father and sister had miraculous escapes. She was well known in the district where she resided, her father being engineer on an estate. A Service chaplain conducted the simple service at the old-world church, and the coffin was covered with the Union Jack.   9/3/1944

Sign Posts being re-erected near Bodmin with the old cross.   *11/3/1944*

Army's Youngest Casualty

At Falmouth County Court, on Tuesday, Mr. Jocelyn V. Ratcliffe (Messrs. Ratcliffe, Son and Henderson) applied for the investment of the sum of £2,000 awarded by the War Department (together with special damages), for Oliver John Bettinson, aged 12, described as "youngest casualty in the British Army", for the loss of his right arm and eye. His Honour Judge Scobell Armstrong agreed to the application. Young Bettinson, on May 29th last, when stationed at a military school, picked up a hand grenade on a beach and it exploded, causing the injuries. His home address is at 25, Bowles-road, Falmouth. His father, Wm. Henry Bettinson, is a gunner in the R.A., his brother, Ernest, is also in the R.A., and his brother, Nimrod, is in the Gordon Boys' Home, Woking.   9/3/1944

Cabbage Dehydration

The Milk Marketing Board's factory at a town in the S-W. is to undertake the dehydration of cabbage from September next. The county horticultural superintendent, told a *West Briton* reporter: "Some growers view with mixed feelings the dehydration of vegetables, but in view of the very great demand by the Forces and liberated countries the dehydration of vegetables is sound business in wartime. Complaints are often received that cabbage and other crops are wasted because there is no outlet for this product. Dehydration gives the grower an assured market for these brassicas.   16/3/1944

Happy-Go-Lucky – Rabbit Transactions Infringe Order

"You people go on in a very happy-go-lucky way: You know there are regulations, and you don't trouble to find out," observed the Chairman, (Col. Stanley Smith), at West Powder Police Court, at Truro, on Saturday, when five defendants answered charges relating to the buying and selling of rabbits… Prosecuting for the Ministry of Food, Mr. R. L. Frank, said Wimberley had been buying rabbits from Goodman at 11d. per lb. when the proper price was 9d. The Rabbits Order provided that the maximum price of a first-hand sale was 9d. a lb… In the case of the firm of Jesse Robinson, he was not a collector, and therefore was not entitled to sell them without a licence. He told Mr. Askew, enforcement inspector of the Ministry, that he bought from trappers in the district, and that he had no licence. He was quite straightforward about it. The firm paid him 11½d. a lb., and he paid the trappers 11d. a lb., less carriage. He did not know at the time that a collector's licence was necessary. He had discontinued the business as soon as he realised he was doing wrong.

The fines varied between 10 and 15 shillings on each charge with costs.   16/3/1944

Mid-day Meals

St. Day School, comprising mixed and infants' departments, was the first in Camborne-Redruth education district to be provided with a school canteen for the preparation and cooking of mid-day meals for the scholars, and when the first anniversary of its installation was celebrated on Friday, tributes were paid to the great value of the provision, resulting in the improved physique of the children.

The hot mid-day meal is undoubtedly proving a great boon, and is so popular that about 75 per cent of the scholars remain to dinner. During the past year the number of meals served has averaged 175 per day, the highest total for any one day being 198. The meals are prepared and cooked in a room on the school premises set aside for the purpose by a staff of four women, and the type of meal varies from day to day. The cost per child is 5d a meal, or 4d each when three or more members of the same family participate…

Many children are also supplied with milk with their meal, which consists of two excellently-prepared courses. 23/3/1944

Fourburrow Hounds
The Four Borrow Hounds were taken out for the 50th and last time at Scorrier House on Saturday, when they killed two foxes in the district. They have killed 54 foxes and three badgers during the winter, and had no blank days. Supporters have reared 13 young hounds to go on next season. 23/3/1944

Night Bombers Out In Strength
R.A.F. heavy bombers were again out in strength last night. For an hour the roar of engines was incessant as they went over the East Coast. They were routed in an easterly direction, heading for the Continent. The German radio last night broadcast a warning that enemy nuisance raiders were approaching N.W. Germany. 23/3/1944

Air And Sea Battle Between Land's End And The Scillies
Aircraft of the R.A.F. Coastal Command, patrolling between the Land's End and Ushant, on Wednesday night, sighted and attacked a strong force of E-boats which were attempting to approach the English coast. The aircraft reported the enemy position and light forces of the Royal Navy proceeded to intercept. In the early hours of Thursday morning they made contact with the E-boats in a position about 25 miles south-west of Land's End. A short but sharp action followed, and in the course of this, his Majesty's ships scored repeated hits with gun fire on the enemy vessels, one of which is believed to have sunk. Other were damaged, two severely, before the enemy succeeded in escaping at speed. All his Majesty's ships returned safely to harbour, having suffered neither casualties or damage. None of our aircraft are missing. 23/3/1944

Death Of Chacewater Centenarian
Three months after her 100th birthday, Miss Harriet Amelia Harvey died yesterday at her home, Buckingham House, Chacewater. She was the last surviving child of Mr. and Mrs. Richard Williams Harvey, of Chacewater, who died at the age of 88 and 92 respectively. Miss Harvey had four sisters and a brother. Mr. Charles Harvey, who died in 1930 at the age of 90, after an adventurous career as a pioneer mining engineer in many parts of the world. When he was 80 he started the Carnon Valley tin works, and he worked almost to the day of his death. The family have been great benefactors to Chacewater… A beautiful stained glass window in the parish church was given as a memorial to members of the family. 23/3/1944

A Record?
A goat, the property of Mr. N. Mitchell, of Tappard, Fraddam, Gwinear, has given birth to five kids, one of which has since died. Mr. F.W. Trewhella (an ex-president of Cornwall Farmers' Union and a well-known agriculturalist) told a West Briton representative that he had never before heard of a goat giving birth to so many kids at the same time. Two or three were the average numbers, four being rare. 23/3/1944

Covent Garden Warning – "Famine" Feared In Boxes For Flowers.
"Cornish flower growers, farmers, and market gardeners who use their own boxes and crates (as distinct from those of their salesmen) for the marketing of their produce should take all possible steps to safeguard them for future use, as the stortage of such containers will probable be much more acute a few months' hence than it is today", said

General Montgomery visits his old school, Kings School, Canterbury, Kent, evacuated to Carlyon Bay, talking to the boys. *26/3/1944*

a salesman in Covent Garden Market, London, to a *West Briton* representative. "Many growers are losing large numbers of boxes because the charge that is branded on them is much below their present value. For instance, a large number of containers that have been in use for some time are branded with a charge of 1s or 2s, whereas the cost of similar containers today, if obtainable, would be at least 3s. Many people, knowing the present cost of boxes and the difficulty of purchasing new ones, are only too willing to keep for their own use some of the returnable boxes at the price branded on them.

"We therefore advise all Cornish growers, in their own interest, to re-brand their crates and boxes and to double the charge made for them. It is not sufficient to write the new charge on the box. It must be branded on by stencil or hot iron… Cardboard-fibre boxes threaten to become as scarce as wooden boxes at an early date. 30/3/1944

Cornish Women Urged To Make More Jam

The demand for jam made by voluntary effort in local jam centres now exceeds the supply, and the public opinion of jam has changed from criticism to praise. This is what Mrs. Lincoln, of the Ministry of Food, told the Executive Committee of Cornwall Federation of Womens' Institutes at a recent meeting, and she stressed the urgent necessity of making jam again this year. 30/3/1944

Oyster Season Ends – Truro Catches Yield Of Over £8,000

The 11th war-time dredging season of the Truro oyster fishery closes tomorrow (Friday), and it is gratifying to know that this valuable local industry has recovered from the depression that set in soon after the last war, which was attributable to over-fishing when there was a heavy demand and a profitable market for oysters. Thanks to the careful preservation of the fishery and heavy stocks of native and imported oysters retained and laid in the fishery by local oyster planters, Messrs. William Gunn and Co. Ltd., Coombe, the fishery has not suffered the same fate as those in other areas, such as Falmouth, where the oyster fishery has become almost extinct… Catches this season have, it is understood, been about 1,600,000, yielding a revenue of well over £8,000 to local fishermen, prices reaching up to about £5 10s per 1,000 freshly caught oysters, as compared with about £4 10s per 1,000 last season. Oysters dredged early in the season and re-laid before selling made up to £6 10s per 1,000.   30/3/1944

First In Cornwall – Solarium For Children Of Camborne – Redruth

Latest achievement of Camborne – Redruth's energetic and enterprising Medical Officer of Health, Dr. C. Rivers, backed by the Public Health Committee, is the provision in an empty shop in West End, Redruth, (loaned free of charge by Mr. James Wickett), of a local centre for ultra-violet light treatment free of cost for all children in the urban district requiring it. The ultra-violet light plant, which cost £100, and which was presented by the generosity of Climax Rock Drill and Engineering Co. Ltd., did most effective work while Tabb's Hotel was in use as a hostel for evacuated and other children suffering from skin and other ailments. Dr. Rivers has offered to carry out free treatment at the new solarium, which has been furnished and equipped.   30/3/1944

"Q",s Accident

Sir Arthur Quiller-Couch, while walking along Fore-street, Fowey, on Thursday, caught his foot on the kerb when getting out of the way of an approaching motor car and fell on to the pavement. After receiving attention from a member of the Fowey St. John Ambulance Brigade, Sir Arthur was able to walk home. He was somewhat shaken and his face and hands were injured, but after a day or so of rest in his room he had fully recovered.   30/3/1944

Bought Ship's Stores

For being unlawful possession of ship's stores – two tins of corned beef and 1 lb of margarine – Cecil Richard William James Gay, lorry driver, Penwarne-road, Mawnan, was fined £1 at Penryn yesterday. It was stated that stores from a ship had been disposed of to civilians and that the defendant had paid 8s for six tins of corned beef and 1 lb of margarine.   30/3/1944

Croft Fires – Appeal To Farmers

An urgent appeal to farmers to take care in regard to the handling of croft fires was made by Company Officer W.A. Trethewey, of Penzance N.F.S., at a meeting of Penzance Farmers' Union on Thursday. … Company Officer Trethewey said there were times when a croft fire need not have arisen or could have been extinguished by the farmer. The farmer was allowed to burn croft land by law, provided the fire was kept under control and was put out before black-out. He urged farmers to notify the N.F.S. when they intended to light croft fires. Thus the N.F.S. need only pay attention to calls from the farmer. It was not always the farmer who started the croft fire, but frequently careless members of the public.   6/4/1944

Penryn Danger – Behaviour Of Young Girls

Announcing that he had received a letter signed by the Vicar of St. Gluvias… and the Methodist Minister, calling attention to the danger of young girls associating with American coloured troops stationed in Cornwall, the Mayor, (Ald. W.C. Basher) told Penryn Town Council, on Tuesday, that a similar letter had been sent to the council.   6/4/1944

Waterless Parishes

Seventy rural parishes in Cornwall are without a public water supply, though some of them may have a privately-owned piped supply. The total compares with an average of 77 rural parishes for every administrative county in England. One of the problems of post-war reconstruction will be to provide a piped water supply to every Cornish village that is at present without one. Such a task will take some years to complete, as there are some 2,596 rural parishes in England with no public or private water supply. 6/4/1944

Sun Drying Cornish Pitchers

Cornish pitchers *were* being sun dried, prior to firing in the yard of Messrs. W.H. Lake and Son, Ltd., Chapel-hill Pottery, Truro, where the 200 year old kiln can be seen in the background. Due to the shortage of metal, there is a big demand for the pitchers and preserving pans… These have remained constant in style for centuries, and the British Council have chosen a range of Messrs. Lake's designs for an exhibition which is touring the United States.   6/4/1944

Not Since 1918 – Very Few Visitors

Cornwall spent, last weekend, the quietest and most featureless Easter since 1918. Of the holiday in that crucial year of the first World war the *West Briton* reported: "There was no holiday spirit abroad; such a thing was not possible in times so full of anxiety". This year the ban on travel had much to do with subduing any notable evidences of a festive spirit. The police were active checking people coming into the restricted area. At Newquay, which is in the area, the beaches and cliffs were practically deserted. Would-be visitors were stopped and interrogated on the railway station and some had orders to go back to their homes. Cancellation of bookings were numerous, and some hotel-keepers suffered severely. There were many visitors to Padstow and other seaside places between there and Bude, which is a "free" zone. One young man who defied the Order prohibiting persons from entering a restricted area was fined at Penzance and put on the next train to the Midlands.   13/4/1944

More Dwellings – Glad About Prefabrication

Falmouth Trades Council have been informed by Major M. Petherick, M.P. for the Falmouth – Penryn Division, that he is in agreement with members that a definite policy on housing is necessary. Knowing how terribly short in supply houses were, and realising that it would be much worse after the war, he was very glad to hear that the Government intended to go in for prefabricated houses on a large scale.   13/4/1944

Mounted Gymkhana Of Western Pony Club

Organised by the Western Hunt Pony Club, with the assistance of Penance and District Red Cross Horse Show Committee, a mounted gymkhana, held at the Mennaye Fields, Penzance on Easter Monday afternoon, attracted a crowd of well over two thousand people, and it is anticipated that some £150 will be handed over to the West Cornwall Hospital Appeal Fund.   13/4/1944

Americans Entertain

Coloured American troops stationed in Cornwall, gave a concert in the Church Hall, Chacewater, last week. A comedy entitled *A Yank in Britain* was highly appreciated by a crowded audience. A boxing exhibition was also given. The artistes were thanked by Rev. H.H. Daws, who presided. A collection in aid of Redruth Hospital realised £5.

13/4/1944

Out Of The Frying Pan…

… But not into the fire. That must be the rule for chop bones. No bones from meat, game or poultry, no matter how small, should be burnt, because none is too tiny to be of use in the war effort. Bones make glue, lubricating oil, explosive, animal feed and fertiliser – all vital to the nation. What Do I Do…?

I save all meat, game or poultry bones from the family meals and put them out for salvage in a ventilated container, such as an old saucepan – or put them in a street bone-bin if these are provided by my local authority. I remember that bones can be kept sweet while waiting collection by cleaning off any odd pieces of fat or gristle, and by drying them on top of the stove, in front of the fire, or in an oven still warm after cooking. Issued by the Ministry of Information.

13/4/1944

Shared A Pig

Fines of four guineas each, with an advocate's fee of one guinea each, were imposed at West Penwith Sessions, yesterday, on Edward Francis Varker and Edward Stone, both of

Newquay Theatre. "Hands across the Sea" Ball. Children with "Uncle" and crowd. The children had just carried in a United States dolls house. 24/4/1944

St. Hilary, for illegally causing a pig to be slaughtered. A charge against Charles Polglase, also of St. Hilary, of killing the pig, was dismissed under the Probation of Offenders Act. Mr. R.L. Frank, Truro, prosecuting for the Ministry of Food, said he did not press the charge against Polglase, whose offence may well have been unwitting, but Varker and Stone knew what they were about, having applied for a licence to kill a pig, which had been refused… For the defence, Mr. E. Thomas pointed out that the men had not given away or sold any of the pig. Stone was an agricultural worker, and they would not have committed any offence had Varker also been one. They had been keeping the pig for about three months. It was very unfortunate and foolish that they should have taken the law into their own hands. 20/4/1944

Asylum For Jews
A resolution urging the Government to afford asylum in the United Kingdom to such Jews as can escape from their threatened extermination on the Continent, and to use its influence with the Governments of the Dominions, the Allied and neutral nations to provide similar refuge, was passed at Pydar Ruri-decanal Conference, at St. Columb, on Tuesday, when there was a large attendance of the clergy and laity. The resolution is to be sent to the Prime Minister, the Home Secretary, the M.P. for North Cornwall, the Archbishop and the Bishop. 20/4/1944

Prisoners Of War
Sir – As push cycles are not taxed and many say they would not mind paying a tax, may I suggest all cyclists give half a crown a year to Cornwall Prisoners of War Food Parcels Fund. Our prisoners are greatly in need of food parcels. If all cyclists thought of the plight of these men, remembering each is very dear to someone, they would, I believe, give willingly. If Cornwall started this way of helping, other counties would probably follow the example. Let us live up to our motto –"One and All".
                    Yours faithfully, Worker for the Fund.   27/4/1944

Cornish People Abroad
"During the years I spent as a missionary in West Africa I looked forward eagerly to receiving my copy of The West Briton each week. Like many other Cornish people abroad, I used to read the paper from cover to cover until I could repeat not only the news of local happenings, but even the price of day-old chicks." – The Rev. W.T. Harris, speaking at Bolingey Methodist Church on Friday. 27/4/1944

Holman Concert Raise £100 For Hospital
As a result of two delightful concerts, organised by the Holman Musical Society, in the Holman Canteen, Camborne, on Sunday afternoon and evening, £100 has been forwarded to the extension and maintenance appeal fund for Camborne-Redruth Hospital. An anonymous donor defrayed half the fee of Miss Isobel Baillie (B.B.C., London and British Concerts), the eminent soprano, who was the guest artiste , and to reach the target figure of £100 a small sum was voted by the committee from funds of the society. Altogether Miss Baillie rendered 27 songs, and her singing was superb.
Mr. W.O. Mitchell (organist of Wesley Chapel), was her accompanist.   27/4/1944

£4 13s 6d For Egg
St. Martin-in-Meneage held its first parish gift sale and athletic sports on behalf of the Red Cross Fund, on Saturday, and it is anticipated that the total raised will be between £230 and

U.S. troops passing through Mawnan Smith, near Falmouth, passing the "Red Lion" going to D-Day exercises at Trebah. All over Cornwall and Devon secret exercises were going on in preparation for D-day.   *Sometime in April or May,1944*

£240… In the evening Mr. Jose Collins sold by auction live stock, farm produce and articles which raised good prices, several giving their purchases back for re-sale. An egg laid during the sale was repeatedly put up for re-sale, and realised £4 13s 6d. The auctioneer reminded those present of the magnificent work the Red Cross was doing, saying that one of his sons who was wounded had written home praising the Red Cross.   27/4/1944

Folk Dance Party
More than 50 enthusiastic dancers were present at a day of Morris, sword and country dancing at the County School, Truro, on Saturday. It was taken by Mrs. Grant, staff teacher of the English Folk Dance and Song Society, and Devon branch teacher and organiser. The gathering represented a very large number of people who are interested in the subject, and, as many of them were teachers, the influence will spread among their pupils. Cornwall Education Committee encourages the teaching of this truly English dancing, which the society considers to be the children's heritage… Much interest is already manifest in this event, which is the afternoon attraction of the final day of "Salute The Soldier" week.   4/5/1944

Bowls In Full Swing
The bowling season in Cornwall is now in full swing and the enthusiasm displayed at the opening ceremonies of several clubs during the past week indicates the present popularity of the game in the county. Denial of the suggestion that it was wrong to play bowls in time of war was forthcoming from the President (Mr. W.T. Tiddy) at the formal opening, in Victoria Park, of Redruth bowling green for the season's play, on Saturday.   4/5/1944

War Memorials

The hope that Camborne – Redruth memorial or memorials of the war would consist not of granite structures, but of swimming baths or some other provisions which would prove of particular benefit to young people, in recognition of the great sacrifices made by youth in the conflict, was expressed by Mr. C.A. Mitchell (hon. treasurer) at a meeting of Camborne-Redruth Trade Council, on Thursday.   4/5/1944

Microscopes For Russia

Sir – As the result of an appeal from me for microscopes for use by the Soviet Army Veterinary Corps., thirty-four have been received, and I should like to express most grateful thanks to the generous donors. As three of the microscopes were received without any names or addresses, and the postmarks are undecipherable, would the donors be good enough to accept this letter as expressing the grateful thanks of the R.S.P.C.A. for this valuable assistance.

Yours faithfully, Robert Gower.   11/5/1944

U.S.A. And South Devons

By the South Devon Flock council, at Plymouth, on Thursday, Mr. W. Colwill, in the chair, *said that* an application for particulars of South Devon sheep was received from Montana, U.S.A., and the secretary reported he had sent photographs of rams and ewes as requested.   11/5/1944

St. Merryn R.N.A.S. Sea Cadets about to load depth charges onto a Swordfish.   *12/5/1944*

Lovely Sight

"It sure is a very lovely sight, and one I shall not soon forget. I wish my people were here to see it. I guess they would enjoy it", commented an American soldier, watching with obvious pleasure the Children's dance at Helston, on Monday.

The Furry Day celebrations were, of necessity, on a less ambitious scale than in normal times, but the attendance was nearly as great as in days of peace. Over 200 children from schools in the town maintained the age-old tradition of dancing through the streets to the haunting strains of the Furry played by Helston Band. It was feared that there might be difficulty in securing enough trained musicians to make a band, but a splendid body of bandsmen, including a postman in uniform, were got together to maintain a custom which has made Helston famous throughout the English–speaking world.   11/5/1944

Youth Rally At St. Austell

The Boys' Brigade were inspected by Capt. Fredenburger, of U.S.Army, at the parade at the recreation Ground last week.   18/5/1944

Madron May Revels

At the Madron May-time Revels, on Friday, Miss Jean Hunt was crowned as May Queen by her predecessor, Miss Cordelia James. Little Mary Hall acted as crown-bearer, whilst the attendants were the Misses W. King, B. Semmons, and T. Nicholls, and pages Masters S. Nicholls and J. Thomas. Following the crowning, the queen released pigeons carrying messages of peace and goodwill to the neighbouring villages. Maypole dancing by the children was under the direction of Mr. and Mrs. J.W. Reed, whilst for the country dancing the children were trained by the Misses C. Mumford and E. Symons. Mr. Reed was M.C. The queen led her procession through the village, which was thronged with local people and visitors.   18/5/1944

"Pride Of Fowey"

Sir Arthur Quiller-Couch was buried on Monday at Fowey Cemetery, in a grave on the higher side from which there is a magnificent view of the estuary waters in their sylvan frame. There was a large congregation at Fowey Parish Church, where the Vicar, the Rev W. Ravely Guest conducted the funeral service and the Bishop of Truro, Dr. J.W. Hunkin, gave the address… Immediately behind the coffin, which was borne by six sailors, walked Sir Arthur's old friend, his gardener and boatman, Mr. J. Welch, dressed in brown corduroy trousers and a blue jacket, and carrying purple lilac in one hand and in the other a bunch of red valerian flowers which "Q" once symbolised as "the Pride of Fowey".   18/5/1944

A Good Catch

A bass weighing 7 lbs. 10 ozs. was caught at Porth Joke, near Crantock, on Sunday, by Sergt. J.R. Bryant, R.A. Using only light tackle, Sergt. Bryant had a hard struggle, and after playing the fish for 20 minutes, had to enlist the aid of two bathers to land it. The rod would not stand the weight, and one of the bathers lent a hand on the line, while the other climbed down the rocks to a wave-washed ledge and, clasping the fish in his arms, brought it ashore. It measured 29 inches. The largest bass recorded as having been caught so far this year weighed 7¾ lbs.   18/5/1944

Improving Stock

Truro Farmers' Union yesterday discussed the question of artificial insemination of dairy cattle, which Mr. R.J. Richards, (county livestock officer), thought should be of particular value to Cornwall because there were in the Duchy so many small dairy farms of from 10 to 15 acres. The only way such farmers could get on a par with bigger men in raising the standard of their stock was by artificial insemination.   18/5/1944

Magnificent Horse And Cattle Show – Redruth Achievement
In addition to staging one of the finest shows of horses and cattle seen in Cornwall for many years, farmers in Redruth district, in the organisation of their annual exhibition in the Recreation Ground, on Saturday, achieved outstanding financial success. The "gate" yielded £298, and the total gross proceeds came to well over £450. The whole of the very substantial profit will be given to the Agriculture Red Cross Fund, and this will be augmented considerably by the prize money returned by most of the prize-winners.The attendance was estimated at nearly 4,000. The grandstand was crowded throughout the afternoon, and hundreds of people stood around the spacious show ring to watch the judging of the horses.   25/5/1944

Soldiers' Gifts
"There is a wave of irresponsibility sweeping through the ranks of the younger children", stated a school-mistress, at West Powder Juvenile Court, at Truro, on Thursday, when twelve boys between the ages of eight and thirteen years were summoned on various charges of larceny, and breaking and entering . Five have pleaded guilty to a charge of stealing a hammer, seven torches, 90 rounds of ammunition, some batteries, and numerous other articles including a pair of dark glasses, boxes of matches, pliers, insulation tape, gloves, elastic bands, and a woollen hat, to the total of £6 19s 3d, all the property of the U.S. Army. They had sold some of the things, others had been recovered, and they had thrown most of the ammunition into the marshes. The school-mistress said, in her opinion, the soldiers had encouraged the children in the first place, and had allowed them to do and take what they liked. They had given them fountain pens, cigarette cases, and lighters, and large sums of money for very inconsiderable tasks. This had completely upset their sense of values. Miss Margaret Smith (chairman) said the Bench regarded the case as very serious, as the boys had started pocket-picking. The case would be adjourned for 28 days, and meanwhile the boys would be sent to a remand home.   25/5/1944

Nurses And Fire-watching
Sir – I have been given to understand that State Registered Nurses are liable for street fire-watching duties. Am I to understand that whilst people may be lying about injured, the state Registered Nurses will be too busy with their stirrup pumps to attend to the injured? The highest degree of nursing skill would be required for nursing the casualties, and this cannot be obtained from nurses who may have to carry out fire-watching duties, in addition to their normal duty. In the interest of the community the fire-watching order, as it affects nurses, should be annulled. Yours faithfully,

W.J. Wills.

Reskadinnick, Camborne   25/5/1944

Double Ring Wedding
An unusual wedding took place at Newquay Wesley Church, on Saturday. The double ring ceremony, popular in America, was conducted by Capt. Boren, U.S. Army. The bridegroom was M/Sergt. Harrod W. Robertson, U.S.Army, son of Mr. and the late Mrs. G.W. Robertson, of Salisbury, Maryland, U.S.A., and the bride, Miss Kathleen C. Wilton,

Swanvale, Falmouth, bomb damage caused by between 16 to 30 tonnes of bombs dropped by the Luftwaffe planes on Falmouth and surrounding areas, The oil storage depot was damaged and the petrol caught fire and ran down the streets.This was the last air raid on Cornwall.   *30/5/1944*

daughter of Mr. and Mrs. R.H. Wilton, The Bungalow, Lewinnick Cove, Pentire, Newquay. The bride, given away by her former employer, Mr. G. Hawke Thomas, wore a white tailored suit of Indian silk and headdress of red and white carnations, and a spray of red and white carnations. She was attended by her four-year-old niece, Kay Vardon, and her three-year-old nephew, Brian Bicknell.   25/5/1944

Local News – Mevagissey
Potato lifting has started in the district last week, and fairly good crops are being raised. Hay-making has also started and average crops are being harvested.   1/6/1944

A Holiday At Home
Restrictions on travelling induced many people in Cornwall to spend the Whitsun holiday exploring the pleasures of the countryside near their homes. Children who found a pond or a stream in which to dabble seemed to wish for nothing better.

   1/6/1944

Cottage Rents – Kerrier Decision
Necessity for economic rents to be charged for houses being erected in the district for agricultural workers, was stressed at a meeting of Kerrier Rural Council, on Saturday, when it was decided by a very large majority to fix the rental of 12s each per week, exclusive of rates, for the two dwellings at Nancegollan.   8/6/1944

In Carriage And Pair

For the first time since 1917 a judge at Cornwall Assizes rode to church on Tuesday at Bodmin in a carriage and pair instead of in a motor car. The Judge was Mr. Justice Lawrence, and the High Sheriff (Mr. Michael P. Williams) brought back into commission the same carriage as was provided for the then judge by his father, Mr. P.D. Williams, when he was High Sheriff in 1903.   8/6/1944

Rope Broke – East Pool Tragedy

The fatality at East Pool and Agar Mine on the night of May 22nd when Arthur Hancock, aged 19, son of Mrs. M. Hancock, a widow, residing at 12, Greenbank-terrace, Falmouth, was killed outright, and another miner, Edward John Craze, Chili-road, Illogan Highway, seriously injured, was investigated by Mr. Barrie B. Bennetts, (county coroner) at the adjourned inquest at Pool, on Tuesday. The accident was caused by the breaking of a wire rope attached to an ore bucket in a winze at the 1,900 ft. level.   15 /6/1944

The Sheriff's Horse and Coach waiting to convey Mr. Justice Lawrence to Bodmin Assizes outside the Barley Sheaf Hotel. The Sheriff was Mr. Williams of St. Keverne, it was probably the last time the Judge used the coach and horse to go to the church and court.   *9/6/1944*

Lostwithiel Agricultural Red Cross Sale. Master David Williams of Trethake, Lanteglos with his pet lamb in the ring which raised over £100. *13/6/1944*

Link With America

Headmistress of Old Bedford-road I. School, Luton, Beds., Miss Amy G. Oliver, whose home is at Newquay, and formerly of Redruth, has made another broadcast to America, a fifteen minute programme with twelve children speaking to their friends, and the whole class joining in two songs. Miss Oliver spoke to Mrs. Robinson, the teacher in America with whom she has been corresponding since 1939, after seeing her name in the *West Briton*. A correspondence league has been established between the children and parents and four hundred pen "pals" have developed. This was their second broadcast.

15/6/1944

A Village Salutes

Lanner's target in Camborne-Redruth Salute The Soldier Week was £2,000, and the final figure was £5,093. Much of the success was due to Miss M.G. Martin, hon. local savings secretary, who was assisted at the selling centre by Mesdames Darlington and Barrett. For the photographic display of local men and women serving in the Army and A.T.S., Mr. and Mrs. W.J. McKenny, of Bell, Lanner, loaned photographs of six sons in the Army and two daughters in the A.T.S. They also have a son in the Navy and another a full-time member of the N.F.S. Thus in a family of thirteen, Mr. and Mrs. McKenny have ten children serving their country in the present conflict, which is believed to constitute a record. The entertainments during the week drew large crowds and raised record sums.

15/6/1944

The R.E.M.E. Girls

They were hairdressers, shop assistants, clerks before donning kharki. Now, in overalls, with grimy hands, they take motor bicycles to pieces and put them together again. They wire the headlamps of vehicles, grind new engine valves, repair canopies and upholstery. They are the A.T.S. who belong to R.E.M.E., and they are proud of the flashes which they wear on their shoulders – the lightning zig-zag of the electrician, the hammer and tongs of the vehicle mechanic, the horse's bit and chain of the coach trimmer. Vehicles of every description, from water tankers to light cars, come in for repairs. The A.T.S. go over them thoroughly, stripping the engine, replacing brake linings, seeing that the dynamos are in perfect order. They have the satisfaction of sending the vehicles out "good as new". All the vehicle mechanics were drivers before they went on their six months' mechanics' course… A Cornish girl, Private Thelma

Inspector J.H. Tucker (Wadebridge) escorting evacuees from Ewell and Epsom arriving at Wadebridge station. *13/6/1944*

Sanders, of Greenwith-cresent, Perranwell Station, is one of the A.T.S. doing electrical wiring. …She used to be a shop assistant in Falmouth, and has a brother in the Army and one discharged from the Navy. 19/6/1944

R.E.M.E stood for the Royal Electrical and Mechanical Engineers.

Expert Advice Free For Housewives

Make-do-and-mend advice centres, where housewives will be able to get free expert advice on all questions of renovating and making new clothes from old garments, are to be opened during the next few weeks in various towns throughout the county… House-wives are invited to bring any garment they want altered to the centre for advice on cutting and making. … Advice will also be given on mending household linen, and making children's garments from the best parts of grown-ups' clothing. 22/6/1944

Nest In Forge

A robin has built its nest in the hole by the bellows in the Forge at Mount Hawke. In spite of the work proceeding the robin flew to and fro with material and made a perfect home. It laid three eggs and now three young birds are being kept fed. 22/6/1944

Baby On Crossbar

William Henry Olford, of Crinnis, Par, was fined 10s at St. Austell Police Court, yesterday, for carrying more than one person on a bicycle – P.C. Willey said he saw the defendant riding a bicycle with a baby sitting on the crossbar. The child was about 18 months old, and was riding on a loose cushion. When questioned, defendant replied that the baby could not walk. Defendant was stated to have made other abusive remarks. 22/6/1944

Bomb In Garden

While he was clearing up in the garden at the rear of Clark's Café, Fore-street, Newquay, Mr. J. Mallis, 9, Beacon-terrace, Newquay, discovered a mortar bomb, wrapped in brown paper, among debris near a strawberry bed. Mr. Clark, the café proprietor, communicated with the police and the bomb was removed to the police station by War Reserve Smedley. 22/6/1944

Food Facts

Now that our armies are using more beef and mutton than ever before, don't grumble when you have to take your meat ration in pork rather more often than you choose. It is this steady stream of pork from Canada and the United states which is helping us to keep the meat ration at its present level. And this is no pig in a poke. It may come in joints to which you are unaccustomed, it may be darker in colour than our home-killed pork, but it is first-class meat for all that. 29/6/1944

Big Garage Fire

Hundreds of people, on Saturday afternoon, watched the biggest blaze Penzance has seen for a number of years. Messrs. Taylors' Garage, in Coinagehall-street, near the Promenade, was burnt out. For a time it was feared that adjoining houses in Quay-street, as well as Coinagehall-street would be involved in the fire, and some of them had to be evacuated. It was between 4 and 5 o'clock when the fire started, and the whole neighbourhood for some miles around were attracted to it by the heavy cloud of smoke that hung above it. The fire got a firm hold on the building before long, and it increased in density for a time, particularly when the flames contacted oil or petrol. Altogether it

is estimated that some thousands of pounds worth of damage was done. Not until N.F.S. pumps from all over the district were rushed to the scene was the fire at last completely controlled, and the place left a wet and charred mess.
29/6/1944

Home Guard Disbanded Soon?

"We all hope, and with reasonable hope, that perhaps quite soon it will be possible for the Home Guard to be disbanded, and for men to return to a more normal way of life," said Canon H.W. Roberts, senior chaplain to the Forces, when he preached at a special Home Guard service, held at Truro Cathedral, on Sunday. Canon Roberts said that the Home Guard had done a splendid job of work since the outbreak of war. The fact that it had not been used in action was not to say that sacrifices had not been entailed. Men had spent long hours in training and watching at the end of a day's work, or after a long week's labour. The important thing was that they were trained and ready, and this was probably responsible for the fact that they were not needed in action.   29/6/1944

Young Acrobatic Tap Dancer

Marlene Hellyar, daughter of Mr. and Mrs. R.W. Hellyar, of the Plaza Cinema, Truro, gained first place for acrobatic dancing (juvenile), and honours for tap dancing in a competition open to all England. The West of England contests were held at Exeter last month.   6/7/1944

Weeds Instead Of Food

Sir – Within a short radius of Trewirgie Corner, Redruth, can be found four fields totalling five to six acres. In one of them there are a few allotments, taking up about 25% of the ground. The remainder of this field and the whole of the other three are covered with tall weeds which will soon have seeds blowing all around the neighbourhood. A large portion of this land has been badly treated or otherwise left to run riot during the whole period of the war. The food situation in this country would be a sorry plight if such gross negligence had been general, and because this is a small area is no excuse to the owners or to the War Agricultural Committee. The writer has personally written and interviewed the parties concerned on several occasions. One peculiar thing is that the owners of one of the largest fields are the Telephone Departments, and they are un-willing to let unless the tenant signs an agreement to vacate at a moment's notice. The other owners, I understand, fix a high figure as rental and put restrictions on the would-be tenants, prohibiting the lopping of trees, etc. Can you tell me why the authorities do not use their compulsory powers?

Yours faithfully,

W.F. Knight. Trewirgie-road, Redruth.   6/7/1944

Three Sons Gave Their Lives

Major A.A. Dorrien Smith, D.S.O., J.P., and Mrs. Dorrien Smith, of Tresco Abbey, Isles of Scilly, have received news that their fourth and youngest son, Major Francis Arthur Dorrien Smith, The Rifle Brigade, has been killed in action. Aged 22, Major Dorrien Smith is the third of the four brothers to give his life in this war. The others were the eldest son, Capt. A.R. Dorrien Smith, 15th – 19th King's Royal Hussars, attached 2nd Armoured Reconnaissance Brigade, who died of wounds received at Arras in May, 1940, and the third son, Pilot-Officer L.R. Dorrien Smith, who was reported missing, believed killed in action over Arras early in 1940, and was later presumed killed. Their cousin, Lieut. H.A.

Dorrien Smith, D.C.L.I., died on active service in April, 1942. Major and Mrs. Dorrien Smith's only remaining son is Lieut.-Com. T. Dorrien Smith, R.N., in command of one of H.M. ships. 6/7/1944

Damage To Road

A case of considerable importance to agriculturalists came before Camborne magistrates on Tuesday, when Richard Henry Wilson Roskilly, Goonzoyle, Keheland, was summoned for having driven on a public road a land tractor fitted with tyres on the wheels which did not comply with the Motor Vehicles (Construction and Use) Regulations… P.S. Dyer said complaint was received by the police that, in consequence of improper tyres being used on the tractor… Damage was caused to the road when the vehicle was driven down a steep hill at Ashill, Camborne. The front iron wheels were fitted with sharp rims on and three-quarter inches in height, which had been worn down to a thin edge, while on the iron rims of the rear wheels there had been fitted pieces of iron used for gripping purposes when the tractor was used on the land. P.C. Job said pits three inches deep were cut in the road. The Bench dismissed the case against Roskilly. *Archibald Millett Bennett, Trevorgan Farm Camborne who owned the tractor pleaded guilty and was fined £1.* 6/7/1944

High Jump Record

Last year's record for the senior high jump was broken, on Friday, when the first part of Truro County School sports was held. The record was broken by June Retallack, who cleared 4ft 9ins., the record for the previous year being 4ft 8ins. A large number of parents and friends were present, and there was an interesting display of school work in some of the classrooms. 6/7/1944

Cornish Nurse In Normandy

Mrs. Pheby, of The Square, Mount Hawke, has received a letter from her daughter, Gwennie, who is at the Q.A.I.M.N.S. Reserve, stating that she is now with the Army in Normandy, having been in the first batch of nurses to be sent over there. She says it was touching to see the delight of the wounded men when the nurses arrived. Miss Pheby is well and happy, and makes light of the discomforts, but says humorously that she never thought she would one day be nursing in gumboots and "slacks".
Miss Pheby was trained at the Royal Cornwall Infirmary, Truro, and from there gained her certificate as a State registered nurse. 13/7/1944

Ban Lifted – Cornwall No Longer A Restricted Area

Since yesterday morning Cornwall has no longer been a protected area to which access by visitors was forbidden, except in special cases. No arrangements have been made for running extra trains to Cornwall or other holiday resorts, but it is expected there will be many holiday-makers taking advantage of the raising of the ban, despite the official advice not to travel. The protested areas of Cornwall comprised all that part of the county west and south of a line running from Mawgan Porth to Lezant, and this remains a regulated area in which the by-laws requiring the carrying of national registration identity cards and prohibiting the use of telescopes and binoculars without a permit will remain in force. Seaside resorts in the former protected area welcomed the lifting of the ban, and already many inquiries have been received from people desiring to spend a holiday in this part of Cornwall. Before the ban was raised numbers of children evacuated from the London area had been received in parts of the former protected area, and others are expected to arrive today. About 1,000 children, some accompanied by mothers, arrived at Penzance on Tuesday evening, and were welcomed by the Mayor (Ald. R. Thomas), and the chairman of St. Just Urban Council and West Penwith Rural Council.   13/7/1944

It Makes You Think…
In 14 days, accidental fires caused the loss of:-
> (1) Enough radio valves to equip 160 Lancasters,
> (2) enough cotton cloth for 30,000 tropical uniforms,
> (3) enough camouflage material to cover 6,000 guns,
> (4) and 1,700 tons of food.

Secret weapon that destroyed enemy fleet: Archimedes, the famous inventor and mathematician of Ancient Greece, is said to have destroyed the Roman fleet that was besieging Syracuse, by setting it on fire by means of a giant burning glass.

Neglect of the wiring in a battery-charging plant caused a fire that seriously delayed the production of batteries for aircraft and other vital war purposes.

Then he woke up… To prevent himself from over-sleeping, a war-worker rigged up an electric bed-shaker, through a fault in the mechanism the apparatus short-circuited and burnt down the house !

The Second Front is in DANGER of being slowed up by accidental fires.

But most fires would never happen if everyone made certain that their cigarette-ends and matches were really out when they threw them away.

You can't be too careful!   13/7/1944

Lay Preacher Oldest
The death occurred, on Friday, of Mr. Joseph Holman, of 9, Foundry-road, Camborne, within about a month of his 93rd birthday. A native of Camborne, Mr. Holman never went to school, and at seven he commenced work in a blacksmith's shop, at Reskadinnick, at sixpence a week. A neighbour taught him to read and write, and received in payment either a miner's candle or a halfpenny a week. By hard study and perseverance, Mr. Holman became a keen student of literature and other subjects, and a great reader.   13/7/1944

War Stoppers
Every screw stopper from beer or similar bottles contains rubber, even apart from its rubber ring. Millions of these stoppers are wasted every year and yet rubber is a vital necessity of war. Every stopper replaced in an empty bottle and returned promptly to the supplier saves the need for a new one. What do I do? I make certain that I put *the stopper* back in the bottle!
Issued by the Ministry of Information. Space presented to the Nation by the Brewers' Society.   17/7/1944

Mount Hawke – Evacuees Settled
A party of 50 mothers and children arrived at Mount Hawke on Saturday. They were accommodated for the night at the W.V.S. Rest Centre. On arrival they were given a hot meal. Billets were found for most of them the next day, one householder taking a mother and her four little ones, including two-year-old twins. By Monday almost all the families were settled in and appeared to be very satisfied with their billets.

20/7/1944

Lucky Escape From Drowning

Sonny Sampson, aged 12, was cycling along Harbour-road, Porthleven, on Saturday, somewhat near the edge of the harbour side, when his front wheel came in contact with a loose stone causing the boy to lose control of his steering, and he went over with his bicycle into the harbour. Although it was nearly high tide, there was a considerable drop. Two ladies who witnessed the accident from the window of their house, shouted for help, and it was the very speedy response to their call that saved the boy's life. A lifebuoy was thrown, whilst a local young man, Mr. Edward Williams, an electrician, lowered himself down into the water fully clothed and rescued the boy. With the help of some local fishermen both were assisted out of the water. The boy, with his mother, recently arrived from London to Porthleven, the mother's native town. Other than for a bruised leg the boy seemed none the worse for the experience.   20/7/1944

Fraud Unmasked

For pretending to tell fortunes by palmistry with intent to deceive, Susie Evon, known as Gipsy Valentina, aged 34, was fined £10 at Falmouth on Tuesday. Her brother, Michael Evon (19), and her father, George Evon, (60) were fined £10 and £5 respectively, for aiding and abetting. Costs of £2 10s were imposed, and they were ordered to leave the town. Sergt. Morecomb said accused were French Canadians, but they had been in this country about ten years. Before the war they travelled with horses, organs, monkeys and so on. They arrived at Falmouth last week, and on Saturday opened up a shop in Arwenack-street. The female defendant was supposed to be Madame Valentina, one of the best-known gipsies from Madrid. The attention of the police was called to the crowds visiting the shop. Sometimes the shop was full and queues waited outside. The fee for reading the hands and telling fortunes was 5s for two or three minutes, and 10s for a few minutes more, but if clients wished to know the future the fee was one guinea. …The female accused said she could not read heads or hands. What came into her mind was what she said. The people came in for a bit of fun and were prepared to pay for it. She had a father, a brother and two children to keep.   27/7/1944

Killed By A Mine

Ronald Henry Munting, aged 12, elder son of Mr. and Mrs. A. Munting, London, was evacuated to Cornwall with his younger brother to escape flying bombs only to meet his death five days later by being killed instantaneously with a 12 year-old boy local boy, Harry Dale, only son of Mr. and Mrs. H.C. Dale, through the explosion of a land mine. After attending Sunday-school the two lads, accompanied by four other boys, went with a ferret and nets in search of rabbits. The two deceased boys climbed through and over wire fencing six feet thick protecting the public. The other lads escaped injury, being some distance away at the time of the explosion.

A County Coroner, who was two hours investigating the tragedy, on Tuesday, asked Mrs. Caroline Dale if she had ever warned her son about wandering into minefields – Witness – We thought the mines were removed.   27/7/1944

First Policewoman

Mr. W. Chappel (chairman of Falmouth Borough bench) welcomed to the Magistrates' Court on Tuesday, Miss Mary Holland, W.A.P.C., "This", he said, "is a unique occasion, as it is the first time in the history of the borough that we have had to welcome a policewoman." There was much useful work that could be done among the girls and women of the town, and the Bench wished her success in her duties. Miss Holland suitably acknowledged the welcome.   27/7/1944

Farm Sold
Tredinnick Farm, Grampound, was sold by auction by Mr. W.H. Cornish at Truro, yesterday, to Mrs. Johns, Trevolland, Grampound Raod, for £2,150.   27/7/1944

Exhibition Of Models
Built by the chairman of the Truro Model Engineering Society (Mr. W.C.J. Truscott, of Trenwith, Perranporth), a 2½ in. coal-fired, three-cylinder tank locomotive, over two feet long, will be one of the exhibits at the exhibition of models in the Regent Theatre Annex, on Saturday, in aid of the Red Cross.   27/7/1944

Two Cigars Realise Over £27
Two cigars, described as similar to those smoked by the Prime Minister, were auctioned at Gerrans Show in aid of the Red Cross Agricultural Fund, held in the Women's Institute, on Saturday, when £169 7s was raised, compared with about £100 last year. The show was opened by Major Maurice Petherick, M.P. for Penryn-Falmouth. The cigars, which were auctioned by Mr. F.B. Secrett, hon. secretary, Truro and District Red Cross Agricultural Fund, were put up and knocked down, and then re-sold dozens of times before they were finally bought by Mr. A.F. Harvey for £1 1s and £3 10s. The cigars realised a total of £27 3s.   27/7/1944

Children's Gift
Tresillian Council School scholars had a great pleasure, on Wednesday, in giving a new bicycle to the wounded soldiers at an auxiliary hospital. Money for the bicycle was obtained by the children at a white elephant sale held in June. Several of the men in hospital blue, with Sister Grimshaw, visited the school on Wednesday. Miss W.K. Brewer, head teacher, welcomed the soldiers, on behalf of the parents and children. Dr. E.H. Eastcott, Probus, presented the machine, and one of the soldiers thanked the children. A light lunch was provided and served by the parents. As the men left the children sang *For these are jolly good fellows*.   3/8/1944

Holiday Makers Asked To Help
The cheering news reaches this country of the marvellous results of the treatment of our wounded by the new drug penicillin. Cornwall is particularly interested, for on certain Cornish beaches grow the precious gigartina and chondrus seaweeds, indispensable for the production of penicillin. But these seaweeds grow only on rocks below low water, so they can be reached and gathered only during the two hours of lowest water at the spring tides. Moreover, they must reach the drying kilns within 24 hours. Messrs. Selleck Nicholls and Co. have, with great public spirit, undertaken this work. So great is the need for penicillin that the Ministry of Supply gladly provides transport for the seaweed gatherers. Sixteen schools and many youth movements have joined in the work in Cornwall. It happens that the August spring tides fall on the Bank Holiday weekend.
                                                                                    3/8/1944

Evaded Duty On 1,200 Cigarettes
A man who said he could neither read nor write and knew nothing about the necessity for paying duty, was fined £5 17s single duty, at Falmouth, yesterday, for evading duty on 1,200 American cigarettes, and was ordered to hand the cigarettes back.

Bodmin Red Cross Horse Show. Mr. W.P. Williams driving "Black Magnet" First prize winner under 13.2 h.h.   *7/8/1944*

Defendant was Vernon Wilfred Laity, Coronation-cottages, Budock Water, plater's assistant, employed at the Docks. Mr. M. Fenton, chief preventive officer, H.M. Customs and Excise, said the defendant was seen leaving the Docks with a canvas bag. This was examined by a policeman, and defendant stated that he had bought the cigarettes from an American sailor for £3. The duty, said the officer, would have been £5 5s 3d., and Customs were applying for an order to be made on the defendant to pay treble duty, £17 11s.   3/8/1944

Pet Of The Troops
During his recent visit to Cornwall, the Minister of Agriculture, Mr. R.S. Hudson, was introduced to a bull which has been the pet of the U.S. troops, who use it for bronco riding in their camp.   10/8/1944

First Pair – New Cottages For Farm Workers
The first pair of agricultural workers' cottages to be completed in Cornwall under the Government's war–time scheme of 3,000 houses, is at Shortlanesend, near Truro, and they will be ready for occupation on August 19th. They are two of the eight allotted to Truro rural district, the other six being Zelah, Newlyn East, and Veryan, which are well on the way towards completion. Pleasantly situated near the school and the main road at Shortlanesend, the houses have an imposing appearance, and are ideally planned. The rooms are light and airy, with ample cupboard accommodation, and every modern convenience has been provided. There are three bedrooms, sitting room, kitchen, larder, and scullery, bathroom and lavatory on the ground floor, with a commodious outhouse approached by a covered way. They have been wired for electricity and will be

connected with a supply as soon as current is available. The rent is 12s 6d a week, which is regarded as moderate for houses of such excellent standard, although it is in excess of the average rent of agricultural workers' cottages. 10/8/1941

Visitors Sleep In Shelters

"House Full", "No Vacancies" – These are the notices which confronted many holiday-makers from up-country when they arrived at Cornish seaside resorts during the Bank Holiday weekend and set about finding accommodation. There was the largest influx of the war years, and the trains, though many of them were duplicated, were heavily laden. The presence in the county of thousands of official and unofficial evacuees made the holiday-makers' problem difficult when they had made no previous arrangements to get rooms. At Newquay this resulted in a number of people spending a night in public shelters, to resume next morning, and in the surrounding countryside rather than in the town, the search for accommodation. Food, too, was a problem, and there were large queues at the restaurants and cafes. 10/8/1944

To Be Filmed In Cornwall

An interesting film is shortly to be shot in Cornwall by Ealing Studios, Ltd.. Its subject, a popular one in Cornwall for the last twenty years, is the friendly relations between the Bretons and the Cornish Celts. Entitled *Johnny Frenchman*, the film will be based on the rivalry between Cornish fishermen and the Breton fishermen poaching inside the three-mile limit of the Cornish waters, which eventually leads to fights. It is soon discovered that some of the Bretons are skilled wrestlers, and this appeals to the Cornishmen, who would "rather wrastle than ate meat". It is mutually agreed to "wrastle it out", and an exciting tournament takes place in Brittany. Romance enters as a result of Jan, a handsome Breton and a mighty wrestler, falling in love with Sue, beautiful daughter of the harbourmaster at Trevallick. The stars are Francois Rosay, Tom Walls, and Patricia Roc. It will be recalled that in 1927 there was a gathering of Celts at Riec in Brittany, and as a result of a conversation between the late Dr. Cottonnec, a great Breton patriot, and Mr. W. Tregoning Hooper, of Falmouth, it was arranged that annual wrestling matches should take place between the Cornish and Breton champions. 10/8/1944

Morrison Shelters

Sir – We are all pleased to know how well things are going in Normandy and Brittany. It is obvious that the occupation of Brittany makes the chance of attack on Cornwall much less. I am informed that the range of the flying bombs (the doodle-bugs) is limited, and although no one can, of course, guarantee Cornwall immunity from attack, it is most unlikely that our county will be attacked. The risk incurred by householders were they to give up their Morrison shelter is almost negligible. It is far outweighed by the needs of areas suffering constant enemy attack. May I, through your paper, appeal to house-holders to return their Morrison shelters to the authorities from whom they received them, so that Cornwall can assist London in its hour of trial? If there is a wish that the shelter should be returned, it will be replaced in the course of the a few weeks, as new shelters are being constructed in large numbers.

Yours faithfully, E.H.W. Bolitho.
Chairman of the Emergency Committee of the Cornwall
County Council. 17/8/1944

Gift To M.P. – Porthleven Show

Capt. N.A. Beechman's interest in the West Cornwall fishing industry was recognised by a pleasing gesture at Porthleven, on Saturday. After the Member for St. Ives had opened an exhibition of horticulture and home produce, handicrafts, needlework, and children's exhibits, he was presented by Master Ian Sturgess, grandson of Mr. Dawe, (hon. treasurer of the show), with a pilchard over a foot long, caught that afternoon by Mr. W. Hosking, and stated to be the largest pilchard ever landed at Porthleven.　　17/8/1944

Quenchwell Grower And Her Gooseberries

The visit of the Ministry of Food inspector to the premises of a Quenchwell fruit grower to make a test purchase of gooseberries, had a sequel at West Cornwall Magistrates Court, on Saturday, when Ruby Collett, a fruit and flower grower of Quenchwell, was summoned for selling fruit without a licence, and for selling gooseberries at a price in excess of the maximum.

The Inspector was charged 1s 7d a pound instead of 7d a pound. Collett stated that the gooseberries were for bottling and not ripe, she said she did not want him to go away empty-handed. She had to pay £1 and £2 costs.　　17/8/1944

Detonator Explosion Sequel

As a sequel to an accident at Camborne, when a youth was injured by the explosion of a detonator, a Redruth lad, aged 15 years and 8 months, working at Castle-an-Dinas Mine, St. Columb, pleaded guilty to stealing the detonator from a cupboard at the mine. He gave away five and got rid of the rest by throwing them in the lavatory at a cinema in Redruth. – Defendant, who said he was very sorry, was put on probation for six months and ordered to pay 15s costs.　　24/8/1944

A Letter From Canada

Sir – A few years ago, when in the north of Michigan, my uncle said, "Oh, I would give anything to duck my head under Carnmarth shoot". With the temperature hovering around the nineties, I wouldn't mind it myself today, or even waiting my turn with anker and barrow while a farmer fills his barrels. What was it – six pails and then the man's turn with the anker? But surely in this year of our Lord, 1944, David Annear's three pitchers a penny at St. Day and the ankers and barrows at Carharrack are out-moded, out dated, and should be placed in a museum as antiquities. Post war plans must list a modern water supply system for Gwennap parish. Surely there's a civil engineer with brains enough to sell the authorities a plan? Why don't the women of St. day and Carharrack of the tribes of Kinsman, Hensley, Pelmear, Jory, Treweek, Odgers, Nicholls, etc. lay down the dictum, "No cooking, no washing, unless there's water laid in my kitchen." Wake up, Gwennap parish. Remember, Stithians men didn't steal the church tower, so why should Chacewater scat-ups steal the water supply?

John O'Cornwall. Windsor, Ontario.　　24/8/1944

An anker was a small barrel or keg which held about 4 gallons.

Fought Hitler Division

The Duke of Cornwall's Light Infantry have been fighting in Normandy, where they landed by June 23rd and were in action on June 27th, helping to push the salient beyond Grainville, which cut the road from Caen to Villers Bocage. They have been opposed by elements of S.S. Panzer formations, including the crack Adolf Hitler Division.

24/8/1944

Paris Freed

Dramatic news that Paris had been liberated was followed yesterday by another surprise announcement that Rumania had accepted the Russian Peace terms, and would become an Ally of the United Nations. 24/8/1944

The Two Mawgans

It has been decided that the Sub Post Office, known as Mawgan, Newquay, shall, as from October 1st next, be known by the name of the village in which it is situated, St. Mawgan, Newquay. The address, St. Mawgan, will be sufficient for telegrams without the addition of Newquay. The change should prevent any confusion with the village of Mawgan in the Helston district. 31/8/1944

Cornish Farmers Asked To Act As "Hosts"

Cornish farmers will shortly be asked to offer accommodate for a limited period to Dominion sailors, soldiers, and airmen on their return from captivity in Germany. The release of these prisoners of war from enemy hands is expected to take place before ships are available to transport them to their homes in Australia, New Zealand, South Africa, and possibly Canada… It is thought advisable that farmers should, where possible, take at least two men so as to ensure that they have some companionship among strangers. 31/8/1944

Foot And Mouth Disease

An outbreak of foot-and-mouth disease at Week St. Mary, about seven miles from Launceston, has been followed by the usual precautions, and parts of Cornwall and Devon within 15 miles of the infected premises have been declared an infected area. In consequence, very little business was transacted on Tuesday at Launceston market, which was practically deserted. The restrictions have caused much concern among farmers who contemplated selling out shortly. 31/8/1944

Killed By Live Wire

A valuable dog was killed and owner narrowly escaped electrocution at St. Mawgan-in-Pydar, last week. Miss Hilda Jones, residing at St. John's Villa, was listening to the news on her wireless set, when she heard from below a squeal from her dog, a German dachshund. She rushed out to find that the dog had gripped in its mouth a live wire running from her wireless set, and had been killed instantly. Catching hold of the dog, she received a severe shock and was thrown back. 31/8/1944

Cligga To Close

The closing down of Cligga Wolfram Mine, at Perranporth, is another blow at Cornish mining at a time when efforts are being concentrated on the preservation of the existing mines as well as to ensure the future development of mining in the county. About 130 men will be discharged on Saturday, after which the mine will cease to operate. It seems a great pity that the company has to take this step, particularly as the nation is crying out for more wolfram, but they were unable to continue to face the financial loss incurred in keeping the mine working. It is stated that Cligga is the only mine in Cornwall that has not received Government assistance, and that it could have been developed into a great industry if the Government aid were forthcoming. This mine has been producing from 12 to 15 tons of wolfram a month, and its output during the past two years has been between 300 to 400 tons. 31/8/1944

Heroic Frenchmen

The heroism of French fishermen in their small boats recently led to the saving of 30 seamen whose cargo boat had turned turtle. A British cargo boat with coal was sailing down the Bristol Channel when her cargo started to shift, and finally the boat turned turtle, throwing the whole crew of 34 into the water. Some French fishing boats, struggling to round The Land's End, saw what had happened and managed to get ahead of the sunken collier, and by superb seamanship picked up 30 of the crew, no trace being found of the other four. The survivors, now in hospital at Penzance, are loud in their praise of the French fishermen. The mate of the collier, Mr. William White, last year spent a holiday at Mousehole. He had previously acted with Mr. William Blewett, also of Mousehole, in a film called *Merchant Seaman*.   7/9/1944

They're In The Bag

Foodstuffs, spares for vehicles, cement for bridges and pillboxes, …these things and many other supplies must follow our Forces on the move. For this purpose, and for the distribution of goods on the home front as well, every available jute sack and bag must be kept in circulation until victory, too, is in the bag.
What do I do?
I search my toolshed, home or business premises for any sacks which are not serving an essential purpose. I remember that good sacks should not be used as coverings for floors, garden frames or dog kennels, or as blackouts or wrappings for outdoor pipes.
I send sacks which are in good condition, or fit to be repaired, to a recognised sack dealer.
I put sacks which are tattered beyond repair into my rag salvage collection.
Issued by the Ministry of Information.   7/9/1944

Terrific Blaze – Great Wave Of Burning Petrol – Air Raid Sequel

A 21-hour fight against a blazing torrent of petrol, which at one time threatened an entire village in South West England, was described yesterday in an official commendation of the officers and men of the N.F.S. Area 19, for "admirable firemanship". Fire Force Commander G. Drury, Divisional Officer H.D. Cassini, and Column Officer E. Rayns were among those named for their part in the incident. The fire was started when an aviation petrol store tank, buried in a hillside, was fractured during an air raid. Immediately a great wave of burning petrol splashed across half a mile of countryside, and the torrent, flowing at about 1,000 ft. a minute, came down the hillside into the valley, found its way into the waterway of a stream, and threatened a village nearby… At one stage a bulldozer was used, at considerable risk to the American driver, to dam the stream and divert its flow away from the village. The dams were broken on more than one occasion by the pressure of water and oil, but they were repaired by hand by firemen… Mr. Cecil Richards said that Mr. Thompson went round, at the risk of being burnt to death, turning off the taps so as to prevent the spread of fire from one tank to another. The brave soldier of the bull-dozer was continually dashing through fire knocking down hedges, so that the earth could fall on the fire. Two men who deserve recognition were George Watts and Edward Francis, drivers of petrol lorries. These men, at the risk of losing their lives, dashed in and out of the flames removing lorries laden with oil to a place of safety. Mr. Richards also paid a tribute to the War Emergency Committee and officials.
This fire took place on the outskirts of Falmouth. At the height of the blaze my parents said they were in bed at night and they could have read a book by the light. We lived in Redruth, approximately 10 miles from the blaze.   7/9/1944

Cornish Blood Flown To France

The Blood Transfusion Team, in the charge of a specialist, which collects blood for the use of the wounded in France, was at Perranporth Women's Institute, on Sunday, and 103 men and women gave blood. Some 600 pints are needed every day, and this is flown over twice daily, and the blood given on Sunday was in use in France on Monday. The team will be visiting many centres in Cornwall, and men and women between 18 and 65 in normal health are asked to volunteer at their nearest centre. The need is urgent, as, without the blood for transfusion, many of the wounded will die. 7/9/1944

Black-out Changes

Black-out relaxations, to take effect on September 17th, when double summertime ends, were announced last night by Mr. Herbert Morrison, Home Secretary.

Window black-out will be replaced by half-lighting over the whole country, except in a few special coastal areas. This will enable ordinary peace-time curtains or blinds to be used, except the flimsiest kind. There must be complete black-out during a raid warning. Street lighting of a much higher standard will also be allowed. Greatly improved external lighting will be allowed for vital work in docks, ship-yards, and railway marshalling yards. 7/9/1944

Familiar Figure At Redruth

The death of Mr. Adam Flamank, aged 77, of Blights-row, Redruth, has removed a familiar figure from the town. For many years he was a vendor of spectacles, he had a stall in Fore-street, on Fridays, and he was also well known throughout a wide area around

St. Wenn Show and Fete for the Welcome Home Fund. Putting nails in "Hitler's Coffin". 9/9/1944

Redruth as a travelling salesman for spectacles. Mr. Flamank, who had lived in Redruth all his life, was at one time employed by the late Mr. Tom Macnair, furniture dealer, and later was for many years on the staff of the late Mr. T.A. Kistler, jeweller. 7/9/1944

Cornish Mansion Given To Church

Seat of the famous Trelawny family for over 300 years, Trelawne Estate, a mile or two from Pelynt, near Looe, has been presented by Mr. C.C. Morley, the resident owner, to the Church of England, to be established as a home for aged and infirm clergy and their wives. The house, containing about 300 rooms, is mainly Elizabethan and has a 17th century chapel built by Bishop Trelawny. The property is stated to be worth £30,000, and a substantial sum for its upkeep is included in the gift. Future residents will make a small weekly payment. It is understood that about £1,000 a year from voluntary contributions will be required for a permanent endowment fund.

Mr. Morley acquired the estate from Sir William Trelawny, who died in France a few months ago. 14/9/1944

150 Years At Lanherne

The Carmelite Community at Lanherne, Mawgan-in-Pydar, on Sunday, celebrated 150 years' residence in what was formerly the Manor House of Lord Arundell of Wardour, who offered it to the nuns in 1794, when they fled from Antwerp on the outbreak of the second French Revolution. The nuns in 1794 boarded a sailing ship used for carrying corn, for which they paid 70 guineas to be taken to St. Catherine's Wharf, on the Thames, and on disembarking, after a terrible voyage, they were subjected to a hostile reception, being at first mistaken for French subjects. They lived in Portman-square, until two months later they were taken to Lanherne.

Of the twelve nuns who took part in yesterday's celebration, one has been in residence 54 years, and another nearly 50 years. Only single summer time is observed by the nuns, so that when the village is awaked by the convent bell at 6 a.m. it is actually 5 a.m. Everyone in the village has a good word for the work of the nuns and their beautiful chapel, which is open to the public. Ten of the original party of nuns which arrived at Lanherne 150 years ago lie buried in the Arundell Chapel of the parish church of St. Mawgan and St. Nicholas, which adjoins the convent and is known to most Cornish folk as "The Nunnery". 14/9/1944

Falmouth's Lighting

To Falmouth Town Council, on Tuesday, it was reported that the General Purposes Committee had discussed with a representative of the General Electric Co. Ltd., the lighting of the town by electricity, and it was resolved that the company be asked to prepare and submit a scheme for the council's consideration. 14/9/1944

Beer Shortage

The shortage of beer was discussed by Falmouth Trades Council, last week, Mr. A. Napier presiding, Redruth Brewery Co. and Messrs. J.A. Devonish and Co. Ltd. wrote that allocation was impossible. The brewery was working to full capacity. There had been allocations from time to time, but there always seemed to be an ever increasing demand which meant that it was impossible to keep going. The trades Council would probably fully appreciate that it had always been their desire completely to fulfil their customers' requirements. As soon as conditions altered in one place then supplies would be switched to the most needy. 14/9/1944

Cornish Samson

Over 2,000 people were present at Mabe's second annual sports, horse and cattle show, held on Saturday, in aid of the Red Cross and Prisoners of War Fund... An exhibition of weight-lifting was given by Mr. Dick Williams, of Penryn, who commenced by lifting an 11-stone man in his right hand and a 50 lb. weight in his left hand. He raised simultaneously a 100 weight with the little finger of his right hand, and a 70 lb. weight with that of his left hand. Then he raised, with his arms and legs, a piano weighing eight cwt., and two 15 stone men, making a total of nearly three-quarters of a ton, which he kept aloft long enough for Miss Betty Collins to render *Deep in the heart of Texas* on the piano. Mr. Williams last feat was to bend a steel bar in his jaws, and then to tie it in knots with his hands.   21/9/1944

Railway Garden

Perranwell Station garden is again one of the best-kept in the western district of the G.W.R. In a report from the Roving Authority, the garden is specially mentioned. Though the G.W.R. ceased giving prizes in 1940, the Stationmaster, (Mr. J.P. Rogers), and his staff have kept the garden up to its usual standard. For several years it won either special or first class in the South-West. Visitors state that it is one of the best on the railways. 21/9/1944

Posted In 1923 – Just Arrived

A postcard posted on the Royal Mail ship Mauretania by Mrs. S. Goudge, on May 23rd, 1923, when she was on her way to California, has just been received by her brother, Mr. David Tucker, of Holmbush, St. Austell. Bearing a George V. postage stamp, with a coloured picture of the liner, brought Mrs. Goudge's message: "I am all right, and a good many miles on now". Mrs. Goudge resides at 250 Washington-street, Grass Valley, Nevada County, California. Her nephew, Mr. Alfred Tucker, of Holmbush, was one of the prisoners of war repatriated from Germany last October.   21/9/1944

Film Stars

During the making of part of the new film, *The Rake's Progress*, by Gainsborough Film Co., at Portreath, Phillack was thrilled to have Miss Lili Palmer and her husband, Rex Harrison, and Miss Margaret Johnston and her husband, Al Parks, staying at the New Inn. This very old place is down for reconstruction, but it is intended to retain its old atmosphere. The new proprietors are Mr. and Mrs. George Chandler.   28/9/1944

Steel Houses For St. Austell

St. Austell Urban Council decided on Tuesday to make application for 100 steel temporary houses to relieve the shortage of houses in the district immediately after the war. 28/9/1944

First Anemones In London

The first Cornish anemones of the season are arriving in Covent Garden Market. They are grown in the Penzance area. Both quality and demand are fair. Small bunches are fetching 1s to 1s 6d, and the better quality blooms 2s a bunch wholesale. Retail prices are 2s to 3s. Supplies are expected to increase soon.   28/9/1944

Helston got Excited

When the bells of the Parish Church at Helston began to ring on Saturday evening, people rushed out of their houses, some being overjoyed at the thought that either an Armistice had been signed or that some other momentous happening arising out of the war had occurred, while others were fearing that the bells were the warning of a

Two Canadian Soldiers meet in Bodmin. On the left is Mr. William Austin, Toronto, and his son Mr. Austin Williams. Mr. Austin sen., was over here in the Army of Occupation in 1915. He re-enlisted in 1939 and came over here and served in Italy.
The son is 20 years old and arrived in 1943. This was their first meeting. Mr. Austen sen. is the husband of Hilda, daughter of Mrs. Scantlebury of Temleigh, Bodmin.　　　　*5/10/1944*

pending gas attack by the enemy. Soon it became known that the bells were being rung by a visiting party of ringers.　　　　28/9/1944

Milk Recording In Cornwall
The fact that Cornish farmers as a whole are beginning to realise that milk recording is the best guide to progressive breeding, improved milk production, and the elimination of un-economic cows, can be seen in the steady and increasing number of farmers who are taking up milk recording in the County under the Milk Marketing Board scheme.　　　　5/10/1944

Scilly Town Crier
The Minister of Home Security, Mr. Herbert Morrison, is prepared to agree to the town crier of St. Mary's, Isles of Scilly, using his bell providing that it shall be discontinued if the enemy starts using gas against this country. For a number of years the local town crier has been Mr. Wilfred Tonkin, of The Strand, St. Mary's. Capt. N.A. Beechman, M.P., brought the matter to the notice of the Minister of Home Security.　　　　5/10/1944

Undefeated Team
St. Keverne Land Army tug-of-war team, undefeated in 21 contests, have challenged any team in Cornwall.　　　　12/10/1944

School Sanitation And Diphtheria
Rumours that the poor sanitation arrangements at Pendeen School had been responsible for

six cases of diphtheria in the area were emphatically negated by Dr. R.H. Hadfield, M.O.H., to a meeting of the St. Just Urban Council. "There is no justification in the fact for this suggestion," said the Medical Officer. It was true that the lavatory arrangements were of a somewhat primitive type, as at many other country schools, but even if they were insanitary, which they definitely were not, that would not, of itself, cause diphtheria. Immunisation was the best prevention against diphtheria. There was a regular clinic at St. Just, but, unhappily, there would always be a certain number who would not be immunised, and thus there would always be a liability of sporadic outbreaks. 12/10/1944

Galling

Sir – It is indeed galling to see Italians conveyed to their work places by a private 'bus while my own child of six years old, and others, have to make their own way – 2¾ miles on an exposed road – to school!   Yours faithfully,

(Mrs.) M.R. Elliott. Ruanhighlanes.   12/10/1944

The Italians were prisoners of war.

Save The Cornish Hogs' Pudding

Mr. J.J. Gerry (chairman *of the Cooked Meats National Trade Association*) said that during the Nazis' ferocious raids on Plymouth the cooked meats trade had helped to save the day. After those terrible raids a cup of tea and a sandwich was a godsend. One thing which would have hit Cornwall very hard was the ban on making hogs' pudding, and it was due to the efforts of their association that permission to make hogs' pudding was given. Although they had been successful in their representations to the Food Ministry for a higher quality of sausage, the quality was not yet as high as they wanted it to be.

12/10/1944

A Bird Hospital

Forty-five injured or ailing birds have been brought to the R.S.P.C.A. Bird Hospital at Mousehole. This is recorded in the annual report of the R.S.P.C.A., which adds that of the 45 birds, 23 died, and nine were released in perfect condition after a course of treatment. The number of cures would seem to be small, but it is only the worst cases that reach the hospital, since wild birds must be very weak from exhaustion before they allow themselves to be caught. The Misses Yglesais retain vivid memories of some of their bird patients. Their oldest out-patient is a jackdaw, Nigger, who was released 8½ years ago, but who still returns to the hospital on wintry nights and seeks out his former bed there, looking upon it as his home. An interesting case was that of a magpie which was found caught in a trap by its beak. There was no outward injury, but both eyes were closed and he was apparently unconscious. For six days he was carefully nursed, the eyes bathed with lotion, and food given frequently by hand, until on the fourth day he began to feed himself. From that moment recovery was rapid, and on the seventh day he was released. It is certainly a tribute to the hospital and its kind nurses that so many old out-patients come back daily for food and the friendly welcome that is always waiting for them. One such bird, a pigeon, was brought there in the beginning as a fledgling, fallen from its nest in a cave. He was reared in the sitting room, which he still visits, entering through the window and often sleeping in his own basket in a cosy corner. On very wild nights he even brings his wife, herself untamed, and persuades her to stay there too. Phoenix has no fear of human beings and feels safe in the sanctuary at Mousehole.

12/10/1944

Cornish Pasties In Cairo

In the quaint little church hall adjoining St. Andrew's Church, in Cairo, one Thursday evening recently, assembled a large gathering of members of the Cairo-Cornish Association, to partake of their first Cornish pasty since leaving home. The occasion was made possible through the organising ability of a member, the Rev. C.L. Vinson, (Falmouth), and the support of the President, Wing-Com. W. Smith (Newlyn), and the Hon. Sec., Sapper S.J. Bath (Camborne). It was the first function to be organised by the association since its formation about two months ago, and although certain difficulties were experienced in obtaining the correct ingredients to make an exact replica of the county's favourite dish, each member present had set before him a piping hot Cornish pasty, true in shape and taste.   12/10/1944

Famous Dairy Bull

Shipped by special permit, "Brampton Canada's Finest", an outstanding Jersey Bull, has arrived in England after the 4,000 mile journey from Ontario, having been acquired at a cost of £1,250 by the Ovaltine Dairy Farm.

The War Agricultural Committee were trying to persuade farmers to record the yields of their milking cows and to use good quality bulls with a pedigree of high milk and fat content. 19/10/1944

Christmas Fare In Institutions

Cornwall Public Assistance Committee, at Truro, on Thursday, decided that the master of each institution be authorised to provide Christmas fare, additional to the ordinary

St. Columb Home Guard, after being disbanded the colours being placed in the church.

dietary, to the value of 2s 6d for each inmate (including children in the children's homes), and 3s 6d for each officer, and that a special allowance of one ounce of tobacco be granted to each male inmate on Christmas Day, and eight ounces of sweets in lieu of tobacco to male inmates who do not smoke, and to each female and child. Mr. J.H. Griggs saw no reason why they should make an extra grant to officers, who were well paid. Mr. S.W. King, Public Assistance Officer, said it had been the practice for at least 12 years. Mr. Grigg said that was no reason why it should be continued.   19/10/1944

Treatment Of Cancer

Second in the list of fatal diseases in this country today is cancer. It is calculated that not less than 100,000 persons are constantly suffering from this disease, and that of this number some 40,000 are suffering in accessible parts of the body which are susceptible to treatment – effective treatment, and if that is applied in the early stages of the disease, then a complete cure may be effected… X-ray work has proceeded in the Redruth area for some years, gradually supplemented as more knowledge has been gained and become available. The Redruth Hospital has a modern shock-proof X-ray diagnostic set, where the wonderful rays perform what might almost be termed a modern miracle in providing a photographic negative, which is most helpful to the diagnosing surgeon. There is also a deep X-ray therapy plant of the most modern American type used in actual treatment, and so the Hospital, with a radium laboratory and operating theatre, in six years as a treatment centre has proved its value in service and treatment to over a thousand sufferers from cancer.   19/10/1944

Went to Billy Bray's Funeral

One of Perranporth's oldest residents celebrated her 80th birthday, last week, by making six Cornish pasties. Mrs. E.H. Smith, born at Greenbottom, came to reside in Perranporth in 1917. She had a family of ten, and there are at present, two sons and one daughter in business in Perranporth, while another son is in America. Mrs. Smith's husband died in 1907. Mrs. Smith enjoys perfect health, has good eyesight and hearing and a wonderful memory. She does her housework and other odd jobs about the house where she resides with her daughter, Miss M.A. Smith, at Riverside Stores. She remembers seeing Billy Bray in her father's house at Greenbottom. Her father smoked a pipe, much to the disgust of the famous Cornish preacher. As a schoolgirl, Mrs. Smith went to Billy Bray's funeral. She has vivid memories of the old Cornish ways of cooking with a brandis, flat iron and baker, and cloam oven, and claims that pasties and bread baked in these tasted better than with present means of cooking.   19/10/1944

Scythed Two Acres At 86

The funeral of Mr. S. Veal, aged 86, took place at Trevenson-street Methodist Church on Tuesday, the Rev. C. Amey officiating. A native of Talskiddy, St. Columb, Mr. Veal lived in the Camborne area for 40 years. He led an active life to within a few weeks of his death, cutting two acres of corn with a scythe during the harvest.   19/10/1944

Redruth Market

Importance of action being taken in an endeavour to resuscitate Redruth's weekly cattle market was stressed at a meeting of Redruth Farmers' Union, on Friday, by Mr. B.W. Knuckey, (joint-secretary), who remarked that the market at the present time was a sad sight. Formerly there was a remarkably good weekly pig market and a fair sprinkling of cows and calves. Redruth was the centre of a large agricultural community.

With a view to encouraging the market he should like to see arranged there, if possible, a sale of tuberculin-tested cattle. His fear was that unless some action was taken the market would remain in its present condition after the war. Mr. F. Thomas thought it would be a great advantage if the market was held on a day earlier in the week than Friday. Dealers complain now that if they purchased stock in the market on a Friday, they had to keep them over the week-end.   26/10/1944

Death Of 10,000
Great success has attended the unit employed in Grampound by the War Agricultural Committee. Led by Mr. S. Allen, and assisted by three land girls, they have destroyed and buried 10,933 rats from October 20th, 1943 to October 20th, 1944. In the Grampound district of Truro rural area many rats have been destroyed by gas and poison and their numbers not known. Mr. Allen, before taking up the leadership of this unit, was an experienced rabbit trapper for many years. These rats would have eaten 33 tons 8cwt 3qrs and 6 lbs of food, in addition to what they would have destroyed.   26/10/1944

Cornish Bridges Calendar
The Cornish Bridges Calendar for 1945 contains 12 views which, reproduced on art paper, are examples of photographic art and a reminder of the many lovely vistas to be discovered a little off the beaten track. One, a meet of the North Cornwall Hounds, at Gem Bridge, on the River Camel, is reproduced in colour as a frontispiece. The calendar is published by George F. Ellis, Press Photographer, Bodmin.   26/10/1944

Bungalow Sold
Mr. W.H. Cornish, Truro, offered for sale at Perranporth, the freehold bungalow, Green Pastures. Bidding started at £500 and the property was knocked down for £1,195 to Mrs.V. Monk, of London. Solicitors were Messrs. Nalder and Son, Truro.   2/11/1944

Maternity Annex Opened At Redruth
Camborne-Redruth Miners' and General Hospital is becoming increasingly important as the County Council centre for dealing with abnormal maternity cases from all parts of the county. The 33 beds in the hospital's maternity ward and in the large house, known as Trewirgie Corner, acquired as an annex, have proved so inadequate that a second annex is now in use in the grounds of Penventon, Redruth, built by the Ministry of Health through the County Council, for use as a war-time nursery, but afterwards found not to be wanted for that purpose. A large one-storey structure containing 14 beds, the building is admirably suited for the purpose.   2/11/1944

Re-Opening Of China Clay Pits
Mr. Percy Harris, prospective Liberal candidate for the Penryn-Falmouth Division, speaking at St. Austell, on Tuesday, said it was heartening to observe Sir Stafford Cripps during last week-end calling for more exports during the first years of peace. Whilst the Minister of Aircraft Production mentioned ten of our chief pre-war exports, it was a pity he failed to include china clay and china stone, particularly as these Cornish products at one time were second only to coal in the export market.   9/11/1944

Truro Horsewoman
Although still in her teens, Miss Pat Ivey Stannaway, of Truro, is regarded as one of the ablest horsewomen in the West of England. The awards secured by her during 1944 were nine championships and three reserves, 35 firsts, 31 seconds, 36 thirds, and two silver

Lady Louis Mountbatten shaking hands with Ambulance cadet Derek Yelland at St. John's Ambulance Brigade Headquarters, Newquay Nursing Division. *11/11/1944*

cups valued at 50 guineas. 9/11/1944

Coconuts For Christmas
Christopher Pascoe, of Hillgrove, Porthleven, has received some coconuts for Christmas sent by his father, who is serving with the Forces in Africa. 16/11/1944

Gesture Of Gratitude
Thirty years ago a boy in a village school in East Cornwall obtained a county University scholarship of £100. During the past few days he has sent the £100 back for the "Q" Memorial Fund. "That was a fine gesture of gratitude," said Mr. A.B. Lyne, chairman of Cornwall Education Committee, when he told the County Council about it on Tuesday. 16/11/1944

Went To Help Of Tugs
The Royal National Lifeboat Institution has made rewards of £11 to its crew at St. Ives for going out to the help of two American tugs, with floating cranes in tow, in a very rough sea. One of the tugs had lost her anchor, and they were in danger of being carried by the gale on to a reef. The lifeboat stood by them until, helped by a shift in the wind, they were able to get into the shelter of St. Ives Bay. 16/11/1944

Flooded Helston Homes

Sir – How much longer are the inhabitants of the houses in the Lower Road at Helston going to put up with the flooding of the river Cober which, at the moment is again badly flooded and is still rising? Some of the houses concerned have their ground floors flooded, and others cannot be entered without the aid of Wellington boots. I have lived in Helston for about thirty years, and this river has been a source of trouble the whole of that time, and I am told very much longer.

Yours faithfully, Leslie Toy   23/11/1944

Milkers' Success

At a recent agricultural demonstration at Truro, two young men, William Waters, Killiserth, St. Erme, and Douglas Hutchings, Trenerry, Zelah, who had previously received milking instruction at the County Milking Classes, made their first appearance as milking competitors and were successful in obtaining two first prizes, Waters in a class open to milkers under 18, and Hutchings in the open class. At the Liskeard demonstration, in a very strong open class, Waters secured 2nd prize and Hutchings 4th prize. On Saturday, at St. Keverne agricultural demonstration, they competed in the open milking class, Waters was awarded first prize and Hutchings second. These two competitors show great promise.   23/11/1944

The milking in those days was almost entirely done by hand.

Flooding In Cornwall

On their way by rail to a big Home Guard Rally at Weston-super-Mare, on Sunday, Cornish representatives saw that large tracts of the Devon countryside were under water. The extremely heavy rain throughout Thursday night had caused flooding in Cornwall also, but it was nothing like so extensive as that in Devon. The rainfall in Truro was recorded by Mr. E.D. Lean, manager of the Water Works, was 2·13 ins. For the 24 hours up to ten o'clock on Friday morning. This total had been exceeded at Truro on only four occasions since 1899. Low-lying areas of the city were flooded and damage was caused, particularly round the Mill Pool, near the Cathedral. Some houses had four feet of water in the downstairs rooms.   23/11/1944

Council House Designs

Designs for four types of new council houses including dwellings for elderly people and childless couples, were approved by St. Austell Rural Council, on Friday. Questioned as to the likely building costs and rents of the proposed new houses, Capt. J.P. Goldsworthy, chairman of the Housing Committee, said that the costs might alter, even within the next six months, but he saw no reason why the new houses should be more costly than those erected after the last war, especially if local materials were used.   30/11/1944

Xmas Pudding 1944

By Helen Burke

> 4 ozs ALBATROSS Self-Raising Flour
> ¾ teaspoonful salt
> 4 ozs bread crumbs
> 4 ozs shredded suet
> 4 ozs sugar
> 1 teaspoonful mixed spice
> 2 tablespoons dried egg

1 tablespoon golden syrup or treacle
1 teaspoonful liquid gravy browning
1 tablespoon marmalade
8 ozs dried fruit
4 ozs chopped prunes
4 tablespoons water and orange squash to mix

Mix the ingredients in their order to a good dropping consistency and steam for six hours. On Xmas Day steam for a further three hours.
Always use Spillers ALBATROS Self-Raising Flour.   7/12/1944

Veterans' Challenge

Four veterans of Mevagissey have challenged any other four in Cornwall with about the same combined ages of 325 years, to a game of snooker. The challengers are Messrs. J. Barron (78), H. Morris (82), R.F. Johns (85), and J. Williams (80), and they are members of Mevagissey Men's Club.   7/12/1944

Who Eats Horseflesh?

The question of horses being slaughtered in the district for human consumption was again raised at a meeting of Kerrier Rural Council, on Saturday, when the Public Health Committee reported their decision to call the attention of the slaughterers to the regulations governing the matter. Mr. B. Watters inquired whether strict attention was being paid to the question of how the meat was disposed of, and the Chairman (Mr. J.H. Ould), said he understood it was dispatched to London. Mr. Watters; I don't know. Mr. A.S. Rowe said Belgian shops in London had always conducted a trade in the sale of horse flesh for human consumption. Probably the local firm of slaughterers were supplying one of them.   7/12/1944

Record Milk Yield

"Vivendel", a goat belonging to Mrs. P. Pollard, Quenchwell, Truro, which has given 3,000 lb. of milk in a recorded year, and it is believed to be one of the heaviest milking goats in the West.   7/12/1944

Collaborators

Sir – I would like to wholeheartedly support the letters by Sub. Lieut. Harris and some "boys in the Green Howards" which have been published recently in the *West Briton*, protesting against permission given by Cornwall General Purposes Committee for the opening of two of our cinemas on Sundays in order to add to the almost fantastic luxuries already being enjoyed by the so-called "Italian Prisoners of War". These Fascists are apparently being afforded such comfort that one hesitates to call them "prisoners" any more, in fact, "Guests" would be the appropriate word.

Yours faithfully, Norman J. Sedgman. E.R.A., R.N.
H.M.S._____   7/12/1944

Over 700 Toys From Cornish N.F.S.

A wonderful exhibition of over 700 toys made by members of the N.F.S. in their spare time, from scrap material, and destined for war-time nurseries, children's homes and hospitals, was opened by the Mayoress, Mrs. F.W. Truscott, at the Gas Coms. Lecture hall, Truro, yesterday. The toys, which will be on exhibition until Saturday, are of every description, and include four-foot wooden engines, three-foot wooden lorries, aeroplanes, tanks, ships, completely furnished dolls' houses, dolls' furniture of all kinds, wooden animals, games and a great assortment of soft toys. The toys have been made by N.F.S. personnel through-out "B" Division, 19 Fire Force, and every town in the area has contributed to the exhibition. Senior Company Officer S. Westlake was area organiser.   7/12/1944

Great Job Done – Impressive Parades In Cornwall
Formed almost overnight in May, 1940, when Mr. Eden, as Secretary of State for War, broadcast his appeal for Local Defence Volunteers, the Home Guard, as the citizens' force later became, stood down all over the country on Sunday. A number of Cornish Home Guardsmen took part in the final parade through the West End of London; while at home, in the county which they had been prepared to defend against the most determined invader, thousands of their comrades assembled for what may well be the last parade of the Home Guard.   7/12/1944

Dunlopillo Beds Into Self-Sealing Petrol Tanks *for Aeroplanes*
The material and labour used in peace time to make Dunlopillo beds have been diverted to inital war products such as self-sealing tanks. You must wait a little longer for another Dunlopillo bed.
Part of the Dunlop War Effort.   18/12/1944

Clock Fast
The rector of Redruth (Canon W.R. Ladd Canney) considers it ridiculous that the town clock "should apparently always be kept two minutes fast by Greenwich time. We are all able to set our clocks correct now, thanks to the wireless signal. It effects no useful purpose always to have the clock wrong, and if it is done because of the unreliability of the clock itself, it is about time after all these years that the works were overhauled by the authorities concerned," he writes in his Parish Magazine.   21/12/1944

Truro's Boxing Day Dog Show
Truro and District Canine Society's show held on Boxing Day was a record-breaking event, both as regards entries and attendance, and the quality of the exhibits was exceptionally good. There were 422 entries, and 139 dogs were benched. A feature was cocker spaniels, of which there were some outstanding specimens, and the judge (Mr. J.W.H. Beynon, Edinburgh), had a difficult task in placing the winners. Greyhounds, always a popular breed, were good, and Mr. J. Prowse's winner was of championship standard. Terriers were not numerically strong, but they were a good lot, and Irish setters showed a great improvement. The toy classes contained some nice specimens, particularly Pekingese, which were capable of holding their own in any company. The best exhibit in the show was Mr. W.G. Boggia's bulldog bitch, an exceptionally fine specimen, bearing championship stamp. Mr. W. Prowse's greyhound was reserve to the champion, and Mrs. B. Steven's wire fox terrier was best opposite sex… The profits from the show will be given to the Prisoners of War Fund.   28/12/1944

Tarran Bungalows
In order to alleviate the acute shortage of houses in the area, Camborne – Redruth Urban Council, on Thursday, approved a reported decision by the Housing Committee instructing the clerk (Mr G.P. Paige) to make application for 300 Tarran bungalow-type houses… Mr. Benbow said while the council would not have to purchase the structures, they would have to make an annual payment of from £4 10s to £5 in respect of each

dwelling and would also have to provide sites, roads, drainage, water, and lighting arrangements. The rents would be weekly, exclusive of rates. Mr. Benbow added; "They are a decent, well-built bungalow and not, as described by one member, similar to poultry houses."   28/12/1944

1945

Logs Distributed
Wood, chopped by Scouts of the 2nd Falmouth troop, were distributed by the scouts in Falmouth at Christmas. Members of the 3rd Penryn group distributed about 1½ tons of logs among the needy of Penryn. The fallen trees, which were a gift, were sawn up by the boys in their spare time.   4/1/1945

Busy Year For Cornish Women's Institute
A year of useful activity was reported at the annual meetings recently of the Cornwall Women's Institute. The work has included much knitting and sewing, the collection of herbs, raising money for charities, continued National Savings, and some jam making. 4/1/1945

A Happy Year…
In 1945 we confidently expect Victory of our Armed Forces and the return of our Gallant Lads.

Camborne-Redruth Miners and General Hospital

In 1945 in this your Hospital we confidently expect

That each day we shall treat about   100 in-patients

That every in-patient will stay, on average   16 days

If the patient is a contributor to a Hospital Savings Scheme,

then we shall receive for that patient's upkeep, approximately   £2 10s a day

But each patient will cost the Hospital   £4 10s a day

We have to find the difference of £2 per patient per day

Now: This is where you come in, help us this year of victory by heartily supporting all events organised by the Appeal Committee. Join the League of Hospital Friends or the Hospital Guild. Support our £50,000 Appeal for essential extension and maintainance with a contribution, and, please, send it early in the year. Send contributions or write for more information to The President, Hospital Appeal Office, Redruth.   4/1/1945

The National Health was yet to come in with free treatment for all. Periodically in the West Briton appears a long list of all those people and organisations that contributed to the upkeep of the Hospital. This was general to all hospitals.

Merritt's Carols In Great Demand
There was a marked revival in various parts of Cornwall during Christmas of the custom of singing old Cornish and other carols in the open air… Messrs. W. and W.F. Chandler and Sons, piano merchants and music sellers, Redruth, informed a *West Briton* representative that this Christmas there had been a remarkable demand for the purchase of carols composed by the late Mr. Thomas Merritt of Illogan. They had sold between 600 and 700 copies, mainly of Mr. Merritt's No. 1 Book… Mr. Chandler, sen., mentioned that during the many years he had been in business, he had sent copies of Merritt's carols to

Cornish and other people in all parts of the world.   4/1/1945

Hayle Bathers

Mr. Tommy Stevens went for his usual swim on Christmas Day morning off Hayle Beach. The weather was frosty and the breakers were high. Mr. Stevens, who will be 91 next February, was accompanied by Mr. R.A. Kevern. They said afterwards that the frosty sand was much colder than the water.   4/1/1945

Keep Off The Peak

The factories that are making our ships, planes, guns and munitions need all the power they can get, particularly between 8 a.m. and 1 p.m. For every time you use your electric fire during this "peak" time in the winter months, you may be robbing the factories of their vital power. Now that you know about this, there's no need to ask you not to use your electric fire at peak times, because, like all of us, you're keen to help the war effort and get the job done. So keep within your fuel target and switch off that fire, particularly during winter peak hours.

Issued in support of the Battle for Fuel by Cornwall Electric Power Co.   11/1/1945

Nazis Like British Cars

When British troops beat down the defences of Walcheren and overran the island, they found a Wolseley Ten saloon, which had been used by the enemy as an Army staff car. From the maker's identification plate it is known that this car was sold to a lady who resided in the Channel Islands shortly before the war. Evidently some high Nazi officer took a fancy to the car and brought it with him to the mainland. Although the engine had been put out of action by a hand grenade, the car was in good mechanical condition and had covered a considerable mileage, although no spares could have been available.   11/1/1945

Lady Seaton's Gift

Twin heifers, five months old, were presented by Lady Seaton from her attested Guernsey herd at Bosahan to the English Guernsey Cattle Society's sale at Reading. They were sold for £241 10s.   18/1/1945

Did Not Keep To The Left

Another record was created at East Penwith Sessions, at Camborne, on Tuesday, when for the second successive court there were only half-a-dozen minor cases down for hearing by the six magistrates who attended. All the business was completed in about half-an-hour. In what was stated to be the first case of its kind in that court, Dorothy Goodwin, 73, South-street, St. Austell, was fined 10s for not conforming to the "Keep Left" sign when driving her car at the Roundabout at Blowinghouse, Redruth. Insp. Ebbett said there had been several complaints about the non-observance of the "Keep Left" sign at the spot. Defendant wrote that she was not well acquainted with the road.   18/1/1945

Broccoli Planter

Great interest was taken at Camborne Farmers' Union ploughing and hedging demonstration, on Saturday, in the exhibition, by Aver's Garage, Redruth (the makers), of a broccoli planter invented and patented by Mr. R.J. Williams, Treworthal Farm, Newlyn East. Drawn by a tractor, the planter will, after they have been dropped in the rows by hand labour, plant broccoli at the rate of 6,240 an hour.   18/1/1945

Snow on Bodmin Moor. A.A. patrol man, B.J. Harris reporting to Okehampton. Taken at Temple Road box.   *23/1/1945*

Narrow Escape

Mr. and Mrs. F.E. Williams, Mount Ambrose, Redruth, had a narrow escape on Thursday evening when, during the height of the gale, a chimney built between their house and the one adjoining, occupied by Mr. and Mrs. Rowe, blew over, doing considerable damage to the roofs and slight damage to the ceilings. Mr. and Mrs. Williams, who were sitting in their kitchen, were covered with dust which came through a hole made in the ceiling, and were also shaken. Mr. and Mrs. Rowe were in the front of their house.   25/1/1945

Dogs At Night

Sir – It is not generally known in the countryside that dogs, especially kennel dogs, should have their best and biggest meal in the evening. This, of course, makes them more contented and so stops crying and barking during the night. Incidentally, people too, get not only better sleep, but also less distress of mind at the thought of creatures cold and hungry.

Yours faithfully, A.E. Fraser, Major.   25/1/1945

Those Who Grumble

Sir – I was glad to read the letter in last Thursday's *West Briton*, from the Cornish Infantry officer, about those people who grumbled because there was a shortage of nuts at Christmas. It is about time these grumblers realised that the war is still on, and that

85

our ships have more important things to carry than nuts. It is surprising how many grumblers one meets, and they are usually those who have least cause to grumble. Very often they have good jobs, good wages, and no loved ones away. I think these people would be surprised if they stopped once in a while and counted their blessings. It may be a good cure for grumbling.

Yours faithfully, (Mrs) R.G. Knucky.

Gribbes, Stithians.   1/2/1945

Scilly Narcissi – Fetch £10,000 In A Week In London

Winter weather has reduced heavily the supplies of Cornish flowers in Covent Garden Market. For several days daffodils from the mainland have been completely missing: supplies of violets, anemones, wallflowers, and snowdrops are very short. On the other hand, pittosporum is more plentiful. So scarce are Princess of Wales violets that 2s a bunch is being paid for blooms in poor condition. The hardy Governor Herrick has stood up to the weather fairly well, and is making from 1s to 1s 6d a bunch for good quality… Last weeks arrivals of Scilly Isles narcissi were the heaviest of the season. Tuesday's consignment of 347 boxes was followed by 364 boxes on Thursday, but Saturday's total fell to 189 boxes. Nevertheless, the total was 900 boxes for the week. The market price remained steady throughout the week at 4s 6d to 5s per bunch, and the week's supply from the Islands fetched approximately £10,000.   1/2/1945

Gwithian Man's Surprise

So swiftly did the surprise New Year repatriation and home leave scheme for the Royal Signals personnel come into operation that one man on the Chindwin front was called off guard, and within an hour was on the "Repat" 'bus. Corpl. F. Clemens, of Gwithian, went on guard at a Corps. H.Q. Signals unit at 4 p.m., and at 6 p.m. that evening he was dumping his kit in the "Repat" 'bus for the first stage of his 8,000 mile journey by road, air, rail and sea. Clemens has not seen his parents since Christmas 1940. Before joining the Royal Signals as a mechanic, he served with the Devon Regt. Most of his four years in the East have been spent on the Assam – Burma border. Last year he went through the siege of Imphal.   1/2/1945

Cat's Jump Leads To Boy's Death

A 10 year-old St. Enoder boy was killed at Penhale on Thursday, when a cat with a lapwing in its mouth jumped from a hedge and caused a U.S. truck to skid and mount a grass verge. The boy, William Henry Roy Julian, 1 Penhale Council Houses, St. Enoder, was on his way to school with his brother, aged six, at the time of the occurrence.   8/2/1945

Coal Gas

Sir – In the year 1792, Mr. Murdoch, of Redruth, an engineer, erected a little gas meter and apparatus which produced gas enough to light his house and offices, and he was engaged to put up a gas works at the manufactory of Watt, in Soho; at about the same time all Birmingham was lighted, and part of Piccadilly. Gas lighting soon became general throughout the country. Redruth will ever go down in history. A monument should be put up in memory of Murdoch. It would be interesting to know how and where he ended his career.

Yours Faithfully, Wm. Kinnaird-Jenkins.

12, Woodlane,   Falmouth 8/2/1945

Throttle Control

Designed by Mr. W.F. Lobb, Lanhadron, Pentewan, and developed along the lines suitable for mass production by Truro Garages Ltd., who have acquired sole manufacturing rights, the "Truro" throttle control for Fordson tractors is now being manufactured by several firms within a few miles radius of Truro. Packing and dispatch are done by part-time labour, and over 100 controls a week are leaving the Truro Garages Ltd., premises. The Government, after exacting tests at the National Institute of Agricultural Engineering, authorised Truro Garages Ltd., to manufacture 6,000 controls. Demand has far exceeded production, which has been "stepped up" several times since the device went into production seven weeks ago. Many War Agricultural Executive Committees throughout the country have purchased them for their own tests. 8/2/1945

As Bombing Range

Disapproval of the Admiralty's proposal to purchase 12 square miles of Bodmin Moor for use as a bombing range after the war, has been expressed by the East Cornwall Planning Committee, in view of the fact that several authorities have their water shed on the land. The committee has asked the Admiralty that a conference should be arranged – The Planning Officer (Mr. G.C. Page) pointed out that the county had made itself one of the finest holiday centres in the whole country, and that part of Bodmin Moor containing the highest "mountain" had an attraction of its own. Presumably the land would be enclosed. There were many interesting archaeological features also.   22/2/1945

Replanting Woodlands

A plea for maintaining our national or semi-national woodlands, a good deal of which had been felled during the war, was made by the Bishop of Truro, on Tuesday, in the course of a debate in the House of Lords on afforestation. These woods, said Dr. Hunkin, should be replanted quickly with the same kind of trees – hardwood beech, oak, and birch, with alder on fen and marshlands. Many of our important woods were small, and proper maintenance of these, he hoped, would be assisted and encouraged. Best scientific advice should be available for all.   22/2/1945

Cornwall's Record Early In The War

Sir Hugh (Elles) thanked those who had worked in the complicated and extensive system of Civil Defence for the unfailing support he had received during a difficult and anxious time. At one period they had 340,000 people coming officially into the area, and at least 150,000 must have come on their own. That was only one example of the difficulties which they had overcome during the past five years. When he started, this was considered a safe area, and he did not suppose anyone thought in 1939 that within two years Cornwall would, in two months, have been the "best bombed county" in the whole of these islands. But that was a fact, and history would testify to the value of the voluntary effort of citizens in defence of their own land.   22/2/1945

Tar Ablaze

But for the prompt assistance of the N.F.S. a fire which broke out at Tresillian, on Tuesday, might have had serious consequences. A huge mixer, supported by four wooden stands, and belonging to Cornwall County Council Tar Depot, was menaced by tar, which overflowed from a boiler, and ignited. The stands were threatened, and had they given way the whole structure would have toppled to the ground. Truro N.F.S. received a call at 12.20 p.m., and, under Senior Company Officer L.J. Stanbury, were on the spot before 12.28 p.m. They were equipped with two pumps and a foam tender. The foam was allowed to play on to the tar, which had already set fire to the stands. The fire was soon out, and only superficial damage was done, mainly to the engine which had worked the mixer. The mixer, which stands about 30 feet high, is used in the production of asphalt. 1/3/1945

1945 Season

The Newquay Publicity Committee is unable to publish a Town Guide for 1945 owing to war-time restrictions. In view, however, of the large number of applications for accommodation being received, it is proposed to produce a Folder on the lines of the old Apartments Supplement, giving the briefest details of Accommodation available. The Folder will run to an issue of 20,000, and will be sent to all applicants, together with an Editorial Supplement as appearing in the 1939 Guide. The space available will only permit of a very brief advertisement from each establishment, and prices will be as follows:- Hotels, £6: Private Hotels and Boarding Houses, £4: Appartments houses, 10s. The closing date will be March 17th, and it is hoped that all advertisers will co-operate by placing orders for advertisements with E.H. Trembath, Central chambers, as soon as possible, and by paying cash with order. 1/3/1945

War On Mosquito

Sergt.-Major E.W. Hague, who has just returned to this country from Burma to tell people how the 14th Army is fighting disease, is to address Ministry of Information meetings at Perranporth and St. Austell, on March 12th and 14th. A member of an R.A.M.C. Field Hygiene Unit, Sergt.-Major Hague will describe how continuous war is waged on the mosquito, which at one time caused more casualties than the Japs. Both are being defeated. Sergt.-Major Hague will also talk about the evacuation of wounded from the fighting line. 8/3/1945

Wallet Washed Up

While returning from duty, on Thursday, Auxiliary Coastguard H.C. Lugg, Gunwalloe, picked up on the beach at Gunwalloe a wallet washed up by the sea. It contained bank notes and several personal papers, including an identity card and photographs, the property of a Norwegian seaman. Mr. Lugg handed the wallet and its contents to the District Officer of Coastguards, and it is hoped that it will eventually reach relatives of the seaman, who is presumed to have lost his life. 8/3/1945

Trawling For Sprats

The possibility of an extremely valuable development in the fishing industry, arising from experiments made in the trawling for sprats, was foreshadowed at a meeting of Cornwall Sea Fisheries Committee yesterday. The Fishery Officer (Mr. W.H. Barron) reported that in the south-eastern waters trials were recently made for sprats, and catches were landed ranging from about 580 stone per boat down for one day's fishing. The prices obtained were from 2s to 3s per stone. Trawling for sprats was an entirely new feature in Cornish waters, and the trials made were due to the influence of the Belgian fishermen, who now formed a part of the crews of some of the Cornish boats. This new branch of the fisheries was being closely watched by the fishermen of neighbouring ports, and if results continued to be good and circumstances were favourable, it was likely to develop into an important winter fishery. The Chairman (Mr. C.L.Fox), said Devon Sea Fisheries Committee declined by a small majority to amend the bye-law regulating the size of mesh of nets which would make trawling for sprats legal. It was turned down almost entirely

on the grounds that trawling for sprats involved the killing of a lot of immature fish…
Fourteen boats at one port, trawling for sprats, realised about £1,000 for the fishermen…
The Chairman said in February 14 boats at one port landed about £1,000 worth of sprats,
and nearly all were sold fresh for consumption. He had been told that the Government
bought over 100 million tins of sprats from Portugal. 8/3/1945

Carried Away Wreck

West Penwith magistrates heard an unusual case, at Penzance, yesterday, when Thomas
Charles James, of Churchtown Farm, Gwithian, was summoned for being in possession
of a drum of liquid, being wreck, carrying it away and removing it, contrary to the
provisions of the Merchant Shipping Act, 1894. Defendant wrote admitting having found
the wreck and carried it away, though he had not thought it was necessary for him to
report the matter. Prosecuting on behalf of the Ministry of War Transport, Mr Henderson (Messrs. Ratcliffe, Son, and Henderson, Falmouth), stressed the difficulties which
would arise if people did not report the finding of wreck around the coast. If the finder
was not the owner, the wreck must be delivered to the Receiver of Wrecks as soon as
possible. Defendant was fined 10s with £1 1s advocate's fee, and 3s costs. 8/3/1945

New Use For China Clay

Mr. Percy Harris, prospective Liberal candidate for Penryn-Falmouth Division, speaking
at Falmouth Rotary Club luncheon, on Monday, revealed that aluminium can be made
from china clay, and has been during the war. "It is not yet an economic proposition,"
he said, "because it takes too many tons of clay for a ton of aluminium, but the research
department of the largest firm in the trade is most active and successful, so we know not

Clearing up Saltash War debris. *12/3/1945*

Boys of Clifton College digging up Molotov cocktails which had been buried four years earlier in case of invasion before moving from Bude back to Bristol. *14/3/1945*

what the future holds. Owing to invaluable research works, many new uses are assured after the war." 15/3/1945

"Mulberry" Harbour
Mr. N.A. Beechman, M.P. for the St. Ives Division, has asked the Ministry of War if he will set aside six of the pieces of the attack apparatus used in "Mulberry Harbour" after D-Day, so that, if suitable, it may be used for the long-delayed breakwater scheme at St. Ives. Sir James Grigg has told Mr. Beechman that the claims of St. Ives will be considered if the pieces of apparatus should become available. 15/3/1945

Family's Fine Record
Six children of Mr and Mrs. Edgar Cocking, of St. Day, are serving in the Forces. They are Horton, Donald, Harold, Gwen, Courtenay, and Eric. 23/3/1945

Warning – Minefields
The public, especially holiday makers with children, are once again warned that mine-fields, both on the beaches and inland, still exist on certain parts of the south coast and in the Westcountry. Adequate measures have been taken in all cases by the military authorities to fence in these minefields, and in all cases, too, notice boards warning the public to keep off have been erected. There must always remain, however, the odd instance when adults or children may wander into these prohibited areas and the public are therefore warned to keep their eyes open and prevent children from straying near the danger areas. The further warning, particularly addressed to children, not to

pick up any strange objects they may find lying on the beaches, still exists.   23/3/1945

101ˢᵗ Birthday
Mr. George Sellers, of Alma-place, Penzance, who on Tuesday celebrated his 101ˢᵗ birthday, is the oldest inhabitant of the borough. He began his connection with G.W.R. 80 years ago, and he was the first guard of the Cornish Riviera Express. His son, Mr. George Sellers, jun., has himself celebrated his golden wedding, and has been organist at St. John's Church, Penzance, for over 60 years.   23/3/1945

New Rhododendron
At the Royal Horticultural Society's Flower Show in London, last week, Messrs. R. Gill and Son, Penryn, received the society's award of merit for their outstanding novelty rhododendron, "Springtime". The firm also exhibited some of their well-known Himalayan and Chinese species, including their new hybrid, "Irene", which were greatly admired.   29/3/1945

Wilful Destruction
Mr. E.C. Carvolth writes: "The castle at Carn Brea, during the past week, was broken into, glass in the windows smashed, and telephones dismantled and thrown on the ground. This is the sixth time such wilful destruction has occurred.   5/4/1945

Shorthorns Much Sought After
Although trade was rather slow at Truro annual bull sale, on Wednesday, only seven of the 58 animals offered for sale failed to find purchasers. The auctioneers were Messrs. W.H. Brewer and Son. The top prices realised was 75 guineas for an unregistered South Devon bull, Caerhays Peter, bred and owned by Mr. Charles Williams, M.P., Caerhays Castle, Gorran. Shorthorns were sought after, and the best price in this section was 61 guineas, for an unregistered dairy Shorthorn bred by Mr. W.R. Richards, Killivose, Truro. A British Friesian, bred and owned by Mr. J.A.T. Thomas, Messack, St. Just-in-Roseland, fetched 60 guineas.   5/4/1945

"Sailing Season" Opens
The younger generation keep up the Eastertide custom of model yacht sailing on Consols Pool, near St. Ives.   12/4/1945

Gardening From Five To 95
Describing himself as a beginner in gardening, but enthusiastic and eager to learn, the Bishop of Truro, (Dr. J.W. Hunkin) opened the second day of Falmouth Spring flower Show, on Thursday. Dr. Hunkin said he was interested in the great gardeners of the past. He started with the brothers Lobb, of Devoran, the eminent planters, and he was now studying the late Capt. Pinwell, of Trehane, Probus. If anyone could produce a gardening record greater than his, he would like to hear of it. Capt. Pinwell started gardening at five and finished at 95, and all through his life gardening was one of his greatest pleasures. In gardening they could hardly distinguish between work and play. He was glad that in the show the commercial aspect was not forgotten, because it would be of great value to them as the years went by. The Bishop congratulated the promoters –the Chamber of Commerce – on having shown the way with the first considerable show in Cornwall for years, and it was an example which would be followed by others.
    12/4/1945

Too Few Blacksmiths

The question of the shortage of blacksmiths was raised at a meeting of the County Executive Committee of Cornwall Farmers' Union at Truro, on Wednesday, when a letter was received from the Rural Industries Development Bureau, London, stating that additional craftsmen had qualified for the Rural Industries Board certificate. Mr. T. Pickard, of Bude, stated that there were several shops idle in that locality needing only the presence of blacksmiths. It had been impossible to secure one, with the result that farmers had to take their machinery for repairs and their horses for shoeing a very considerable distance. Other speakers emphasised a similar position in their localities. It was decided to communicate with the Labour Committee of the War Agricultural Committee to ascertain whether anything could be done in the matter.   12/4/1945

Lifeboatmen Busy

During six days the lifeboats from Plymouth, The Lizard, Penlee, and Sennen Cove have been out to the help of two American steamers, a Dutch motor vessel, and a British steamer. They landed 49 men and salved two rafts. The R.N.L.I. made rewards to them of over £100.   12/4/1945

About this time Cornish Prisoners of War began arriving home.

Seventy Years Wed

Mr. and Mrs. Brown, of Pabyer, Gorran Haven, will be celebrating 70th Anniversary of their wedding on April 24th. Mr. Brown is 90 and his wife 89.   19/4/1945

New Gas Kitchen In An Old Setting

The "Package" Kitchen (planned for post-war mass production) will be ideal for old houses converted into flats. A complete unit, with gas cooker, gas refrigerator, sink, plate-rack, cupboards. It could be delivered at the door ready for speedy erection. In enamelled steel, wood or aluminium. Practical and good-looking.

British gas Council, London S.W.1   19/4/1945

Those Lost Bottles

A serious position created by the non-return of milk bottles to the retailer was discussed by St. Austell Urban Food Control committee, on Tuesday. It was decided to support the members of the War-time Dairymen's Association, who had adopted a very efficient remedy to deal with irresponsible consumers who failed to return the bottles. If a household was entitled to three bottles a day, and returned two, only two full bottles were left on the doorstep, the association's slogan being – "No milk bottle, no milk". The committee, in discussing ice cream supplies, expressed their desire that no retailer would attempt to exploit the children's coppers, and it was to be hoped they would maintain the traditional reputation of the Cornish trader for fair dealing, both in regard to the value given as well as the quality supplied.   26/4/1945

Worthy Response

Over 200 household articles were received at the Unionist Hall, Stithians, on Thursday, for the bombed-out residents of Wandsworth. The collection was organised by members of Stithians W.V.S. under Mrs. E.F. Gordon.   26/4/1945

Family Free

Mrs. Dungey, Fiddlers Green, Newlyn East, has received a letter from her son, Arthur, to say that he and his wife and family are free after having been prisoners of the

Japanese since the fall of the Philippines. 26/4/1945

Camps In Cornwall

Five Volunteer Agricultural Camps are being held in Cornwall this year. The response to the appeal for volunteers has been good so far, and many people who stayed at the camps last year are paying return visits. Poltair Camp, Penzance, will be the first to open in Cornwall. It starts on May 5th, will remain open until July 31st, and can cater for 50 people a week. The camp is a large house which was previously a Land Army hostel, and the main work is market gardening. Rosteague Manor, at Gerrans, Portscatho, with its secret passage – one time smugglers haunt – running from the house to the sea, proved one of the most attractive camps last year. It accommodates 40 persons a week, and the main work is harvesting and potato picking. It will be open from June 2nd to October 27th. Tyrock Camp, Porthleven, was formally a hotel, and will be open from June 2nd to November 3rd. It is on the sea front, and accommodates 50 people a week. Here the work will be varied, and include hoeing, harvesting, and potato picking.   26/4/1945

Nearly 150,000 Miles Walked

A second link in the association, covering a century, of members of the Exelby family, Redruth, with the Post office service, has been severed in the retirement, on Saturday, on reaching the age limit, of Mr. Richard John Exelby, 1, Trevithick-road, Pool, who, since 1937, has been supervising postman at Camborne. A native of South Downs, Redruth, Mr. Exelby is the eldest son of the late Mr. John Exelby, for about 37 years a postman at Redruth and Helston. On leaving school in 1899, Mr. R.J. Exelby joined the staff of Redruth Post Office as a telegraph messenger, and, subsequently, he became an auxiliary postman successively for Gwennap, Illogan Highway, and Mawla districts. In 1907 he was established and transferred to Carn Brea, where he remained 30 years. During his 46 years' postal service Mr. Exelby estimates he walked nearly 150,000 miles. When a telegraph messenger, he delivered for posting in the shop of the late Mr. T. Roskrow, bookseller and stationer, Fore-street, Redruth, the telegram which announced the death of Queen Victoria. 26/4/1945

Stud Notices

Season 1945 – that grand Clydesdale Stallion, rising 5 years old, 17 h.h., No. 3491, St licensed by the Ministry of Agriculture and Fisheries, will travel as usual: particulars later. J.H. Williams, Cubert; 'phone Crantock 244
Season 1945 – "Godolphin Ploughboy", Suffolk Stallion, will stand at home. Ministry licence 6349: fee £2. S.E. Schofield, Godolphin Manor, near Helston.
To stand at home – Pedigree Suffolk Punch stallion, "Pyrford Pedro", 7160; stands 16·2 h.h.,with excellent bone and feet, holding Ministry of Agriculture's licence
No. 4889 for 1945; fee 35s and 2s 6d groom's fee: all mares covered to be paid for.
H. Johns, Wheal Davey, St. Agnes. 26/4/1945

Trees For Downs

A suggestion by the Clerk (Mr. W.I. Whitburn) that the many hundreds of acres of waste land at United, near Carharrack, might be utilised for afforestation purposes as a post-war development scheme was supported at the annual meeting of Gwennap Parish Council, on Thursday, when Mr. Whitburn was directed to call the attention of the Forestry Commission to the matter. Mr. Whitburn pointed out that at United there were nearly one thousand acres of land which for many years had been derelict. The type of tree which would prove suitable for such land was a question for experts to decide, but he suggested that spruce, Scotch fir, or larch would probably be suitable. There was space available for probably 250,000 trees. Apart from the employment provided, the trees would beautify what for many years had been a blot on the countryside, and would eventually prove a commercial asset to the nation.   3/5/1945

Tamar Strawberries Ruined

Between 80 and 90 per cent of the strawberry crop in the Tamar Valley has been ruined by the recent severe weather. A well-known grower there told a *West Briton* representative, on Tuesday, that the previous night there was a fall of two inches of snow and eight degrees of frost. "It knocked thousands of pounds out of the Tamar Valley", he said. In addition to the destruction of the strawberries, the plums and gooseberries were dropping off, and the cherries were seriously affected.   3/5/1945

Germany Out Of Italian Campaign

The German land, sea, and air forces in Italy have surrendered unconditionally to Field Marshal Alexander.   3/5/1945

Evacuees To Return

Cornish local authorities received a telegram from the Minister of Health:- "Operation London return plans". This was the signal to put into action the plans for the final return home of the Greater London evacuees. The first trains with mothers and children will run in about a month's time, and trains for school children will start in about six weeks. The Order applies to those with homes to go to. Others are asked to stay put. 3/5/1945
V.E. Day (Victory in Europe) was declared on May 7th.

Days Of Thanksgiving And Rejoicing – Truro Cathedral Filled To Overflowing

To-day, after two days of victory thanksgiving and rejoicings, Cornwall returns to work, ready to take its full part in whatever may be required to subdue the last remaining aggressor nation, Japan. The utter defeat of Nazi Germany has been accomplished, and the Third Reich, which Hitler and the Nazis founded when he came to power in 1933, has been brought down in ruins upon its founders' heads. At one minute past midnight yesterday morning hostilities in Europe, which began with Germany's invasion of Poland in 1939, were officially ended, but the "Cease Fire" began to sound all along the front on Monday.   10/5/1945

Team From Cornwall – To Help The Children Of Holland

"As we meet on the eve of victory with all thankfulness and rejoicing, we are bound to remember the cost and suffering the war has brought in its train", said Mrs. J.W. Hunkin, wife of the Bishop of Truro, presiding at a meeting of the "Save the Children Fund, held at Truro, on Thursday. The most important task in the rebuilding of Europe, Mrs. Hunkin continued, was the re-making of the most innocent suffers – the children. They had been starved of love and had seen things that no child should see, and worst of all they had seen those they love suffer.

(*Miss Ferguson, the speaker, said*)… she was sure they all wanted to play their part in helping the children of Europe, and that would mean being able to raise enough money to keep the teams (*of helpers*) in the field. It cost between £3,500 and £4,000 a team. Cornwall had sent a relief team of 12 to Holland. It would feed and clothe the children, find out their needs, assist in tracing parents who had been taken for slave labour, and help the children who were still with their parents so that they should get food and some sort of schooling. The team was a direct ambassador from Cornwall.   10/5/1945

First In Cornwall

The first official welcome, in Cornwall, to a returned prisoner of war, was given to Driver Charles Andrew, of Lanner, when presentations to the value of over £50 were made to him.   10/5/1945

Seamen Outwitted The Germans

VE–Day was one of double rejoicing for Mr. and Mrs. W.G. Hodge, of 5, Park Holly, Treswithian, who welcomed home their eldest son, Mr. William George Hodge, Merchant Navy, a prisoner in Poland and Germany for over 4½ years. In September, 1940, Mr. Hodge was on duty in the engine room when his ship was shelled by a German raider 600 miles off the Azores. After floating in the water for three hours, members of the crew were picked up by the raider, a converted liner, which had on board the crew of another British tanker. His first nine months in Poland were the hardest of his confinement. He saw many seamen cry with joy on receiving his first Red Cross parcel. With the Germans the seamen were able to exchange soap and cigarettes for parts of wireless sets, from which the main set of the camp was cleverly built and hidden in a butcher's block. When the Germans realised the liberation of the camp was imminent, they tried to force march about 600 Royal Navy, Marines, and R.A.F. prisoners to Lubeck. Through the efforts of the merchant seamen, this attempt was a great failure, as they hid 500 of the Naval men by burying them in the sandy soil and covering their heads over with boxes, and others were placed in the bottom of the seamen's bunks, with blankets over them. *The German guard dogs did not find them as the prisoners had scattered pepper and delousing powder near the hidden men.* Consequently, when the Guards Armoured Division liberated the camp on April 28th, they freed 500 more prisoners than the Germans intended. Mr. Hodge, who was one of the welfare workers in the camp, is full of praise for the Red Cross organisation.   17/5/1945

Mullion Cove For Nation

Mullion Cove, one of Cornwall's best known beauty spots, has been acquired by the National Trust, through the munificence of the owner, Mr. Montague Meyer. The gift comprises of twelve acres, including Mullion Island and harbour, which some years ago Mr. Meyer purchased, along with the jetties and fish cellars, from Viscount Clifden. Mullion Cove has for years been the resort of countless visitors. Mr. Meyer is well known at Mullion where he has been in the habit of spending two or three holidays each year. He is a London timber merchant. Mr. Meyer bought the old boathouse some years ago, made it a residence, and has been a constant visitor since the last war.   24/5/1945

Donkey Derby

A Services' Donkey Derby created much entertainment at Mawnan Red Cross Agricultural Show, on Saturday. Representatives of the Army, Royal Navy, R.A.F., and the W.R.E.N.S. competed and found, to their own discomfort and great amusement of the spectators, that bare-back donkey riding is not as easy as it looks. The show was well organised and there were about 200 entries. There was a larger cattle section than last year. The quality of the exhibits in both sections was very high.   31/5/1945

Potato Blight Appears

Numbers of growers in the Penzance district are being forced to lift their early potatoes sooner than they would have done normally, because potato blight is fairly widespread in some areas. The spread of the disease is due to the recent warm, humid weather. 31/5/1945

Typical Of Cornish Kindness
A tribute to the kindness and hospitality of Cornish people was paid by a London mother, whose children were evacuated to Cornwall. She is Mrs. N. Thorne, of 23, Abingdon-road, Finchley, and her gratitude towards Mr. and Mrs. J. Bawden, Coxhill, Chacewater, who received her children into their home and treated them as part of their family, is unbounded. George and Rita Thorne arrived in Chacewater three years ago and, when George left school and returned to London, Rita, now aged 11, remained happily with her foster-parents. Whenever Mr. and Mrs. Thorne came to visit their children they were invited to stay for as long as they liked… Mrs. Thorne said she believed her experience had been shared by many other parents of children evacuated to the county. She was sure that many evacuees would go home with happy memories of Cornwall.   31/5/1945

Cricket
Camborne defeated an R.A.F. side by one wicket in the last over of the match. The R.A.F. scored 115, a third wicket partnership by Woodman (25) and Hill (62) yielding 73 runs. Godolphin was the most successful of the Camborne bowlers, getting five wickets for 30 runs. G. Holman (23) and J. Floyd (32) opened the Camborne innings, and 99 was reached at the fall of the fifth wicket. After the dismissal of Eric Holman (15), the next three wickets fell for eight runs. The scores were level when the last man went in, and three runs were obtained in the last over, which brought Camborne's total to 118 for nine wickets, George Rogers also contributed 20.   7/6/1945

U-Boat Visiting Falmouth
Falmouth is to have the U-boat U 1023 on view next Saturday and Sunday. The German sub-marine will be secured at King's Jetty, Falmouth Dockyard, and will be open to members of H.M. and Allied Forces and Merchant Navies between 10 a.m. and 1 p.m. and to the public between 1 p.m. and 7 p.m.   7/6/1945

Blackout Material
Sir – I have received an appeal from the President of the Greek Red Cross, supported by the Foreign Relations Department of the British Red Cross Department, asking for black-out material that is not needed to be sent to the Greeks. There is a desperate need of clothing in Greece, and in the summer women and children can wear cotton clothing, so that the blackout material will be very welcome there. I shall be pleased, therefore, if anyone will post or bring blackout material to the given address at Falmouth. Yours sincerely,
G. Romney Fox, Vice Consul for Greece.
48, Arwennack-street, Falmouth.   7/6/1945

No Cornish Gorsedd This year
There is to be no open Gorsedd of the Cornish Bards this year, because of the war with Japan. This was announced by the Grand Bard (Mr. R. Morton Nance) at a meeting of the bards, at Truro, on Saturday, when it was decided that there should be a closed Gorsedd on the first Saturday in September. It was also decided to send greetings to the Breton, Welsh and French Gorsedds. Mr. W. Tregoning Hooper read a short paper on the preservation of Cornish engines, and said Cornwall's outstanding contribution to world

progress was that of its engineers in the early development of the steam engine, which had been by far the greatest factor in the world's material progress. The Cornish pumping engine was said to be the only machine man ever finished. A society has been formed to preserve the few Cornish engines which still survive.   7/6/1945

Soap Ration
The soap ration leaves little over for such essential items as the annual blanket washing, and so in many instances the washing must go until better times. It is, however, possibly for everybody to hang their blankets out in the sun for a few hours. This purifies them and freshens them up before being put away for next winter. Moths are more liable to attack used clothes and woollens, so be sure to use plenty of camphor when packing them away. Moths dislike the smell of newsprint so an outer wrapping of newspapers is an extra precaution against their depredations. When soda is unobtainable paraffin and powdered soap is equally efficient as a grease dissolver.   11/6/1945

Killiow House To Become Rehabilitation Centre
Killiow House, with part of the estate, about two miles from Truro on the main road to Falmouth, has been acquired by the Royal Cornwall Infirmary as a permanent civilian centre. It is hoped that the centre, which will ultimately provide for up to 200 patients, will be opened in the autumn. Under the scheme, Cornwall will be among the first counties in the country to possess a central hospital with an annex for residential rehabilitation of all types of in-patient disability. This scheme is a natural sequel to the present activities of the Royal Cornwall Infirmary under the Emergency Medical Service of the Ministry of Health, in connection with which, since early in the war, the Infirmary has been the orthopaedic and fracture centre for the county of Cornwall, dealing with the three fighting services and also with so-called industrial accidents. When the Emergency Hospital Scheme was first designed it was intended mainly to cope with air-raid needs and to help the services. It has since been developed considerably and now caters for numerous and large classes of the population.   14/6/1945

T.B. In Cattle
"This county is very free from tuberculosis of cattle. We read of 40 per cent of cattle of this country suffering from T.B., and it may be, but not in Cornwall," declared Mr. H.W. Hicks, animal husbandry officer of the War Agricultural Executive Committee, speaking on "Improvement of Livestock" at a meeting of the Truro Farmers' Union, yesterday. Mr. G. Langdon presided. Devon and Cornwall, Mr. Hicks said, were two of the counties most free from tuberculosis, presumably because of the open air life of the cattle. In Cornwall the stock lived under natural conditions, and he was of the opinion that if tests were carried out, it would be found that there were only a small number of reactors among the cattle in the county.   14/6/1945

Its First
A grey African parrot, owned by Mrs. W. Symons, Kudna, Trenwheal, has laid its first egg at the age of 20 years.   21/6/1945

Champion Baby
Susan Dutfield, aged eight months, was champion baby at Gorran Gala Day, held in aid of St. Dunstan's and the Missions to Seamen.   21/6/1945

Tyres Without Permits

Fixed Standard Prices

We can now accept customers' sound Car Tyres for Rebuilding by Makers, and can supply Rebuilt Tyres and New Tubes as supplies become available,

WITHOUT PERMITS.

West of England Tyre Co., Foundry Square, Hayle. 'Phone 2323   21/6/1945

His 43rd Dog Rescue

Mr. Charles Phillips, Fraddam, Gwinear, the holder of numerous awards by the R.S.P.C.A., last week effected his 43rd rescue of a dog. This belonged to Mr. A. Stephens, 45, Enys-road, Camborne, and had fallen down a disused mine shaft on Rosewarne Farm. Mr. Phillips, who volunteered to descend the shaft, found the dog sitting on a ledge by the water, some 60 feet from the surface.   28/6/1945

Thanksgiving

There'll always be an England. Now, England is saved. How can we best give thanks? By making this England a land worth living in. By thrift – by saving. Our savings helped our men defeat Germany. Our continued savings will help make this country worthy of the men who preserved it.

GIVE THANKS BY SAVING. Issued by the National Savings Committee.   2/7/1945

Record Potato Crop

From less than 1·125 acres, Mr. W.J. Watts has cropped 14 tons 11½ cwt. of Arran Pilot potatoes at Narabo Farm, Devoran.   5/7/1945

Yacht In Distress

The 10-ton yacht, Susannah, was recently found in distress off the West Coast of Africa by a British warship. On board were Mr. W.H. Weeks, aged 51, a London dentist, who had resided and practised at St. Ives since his surgery in London was bombed in 1941, and his 19-year-old son, Geoffrey. The yacht was flying signals of distress and the captain of the warship found that the craft was badly battered, with mast broken and sails ripped away. Mr. Weeks shouted to the captain that his son was badly injured, and he was brought aboard the warship strapped to a stretcher, while the father followed. Eventually, with Mr. Weeks' consent, the yacht was sunk by gun-fire, and father and son are now on their way home to England in the warship. Mr. Weeks, who was a keen member of St. Ives Fire Guard, was frequently seen sailing the Susannah in the bay, and on one occasion in a storm he was blown towards the Scillies, where he sought shelter. When a few weeks ago he left home with his son, Mrs. Weeks had no idea that her husband intended to set out on a 4,000 mile voyage from Britain to Trinidad. For some time Mr. and Mrs. Weeks, whose St. Ives home is 3, Park-avenue-terrace, lived in the island of Tobago, and Mrs. Weeks knew of her husband's great desire to return to Trinidad.   5/7/1945

First Polling Day Since 1935

For the first time since November 14th, 1935, the electors go to the polls today to choose a new Parliament. The election campaign which concluded last night was probably the quietest in living memory in Cornwall, though in some parts of the country considerable liveliness has been reported… In each of the five Cornish divisions the electors are being asked to choose one of three candidates… The electorate in Cornwall comprises of 224,967 civilians and 20,463 members of the Forces… Declaration of the poll will be on

Fish Canning Factory At Newlyn

There is to be a new fish canning at Newlyn, and it is hoped that many of the surplus fish which have been caught in ports in West Cornwall can be absorbed in this factory and, to some extent, the gluts of pilchards and mackerel can be obviated.   5/7/1945

Rigged The Cutty Sark

The funeral took place at Falmouth Cemetery, yesterday, of Mr. Alexander Hawk Hunt, 5, Old-hill, Falmouth, who died suddenly on Friday. Aged 70, Mr. Hunt served his apprenticeship with Mr. P. Williams, of Church-street, Falmouth, and for the past 20 years has been employed by Mr. W. Penrose, Truro. He was responsible for rigging out the famous sailing vessel, Cutty Sark, with sails.   5/7/1945

Voting By Post

Sir – Now that the General Election is over and we have a little time to breathe, allow me to call attention to the advantages or otherwise of having a change in our voting system. There are many who think the use of the ballot could be extended to the post. Nearly everything is now done by this means, and I suppose with satisfaction.

Yours truly, W.J. Davey, Perranwell Station.   19/7/1945

Sunk Off The Lizard

Among the missing members of the trawler Kurd, which was sunk off the Lizard, on Tuesday of last week, is Leading Seaman William Bassett, husband of Mrs. A. Bassett, of 30, William-street, Camborne. A native of St. Ives, he had been in the services for five years and had been engaged in mine sweeping practically all the time. The Kurd is believed to be the first Naval vessel to be lost by mines off our coast since the war ended. Leading Seaman Bassett had been a survivor from two previous sinkings by enemy action earlier in the war. Prior to joining the Navy, he was head porter at the Porthminster Hotel, St. Ives, and a member of the Seamen's Institute. In addition to the widow he leaves two young boys.   19/7/1945

Porthcurno Tunnels

It has been revealed that Cable and Wireless Ltd., realising that successful enemy attack on the cable head at Porthcurno would sever Britain's cable connections with the outside world, sought Government approval to excavate two tunnels under the rock, 150 feet deep, to contain the entire operational equipment and staff. Similar precautions were taken at Malta and Gibraltar, and other vulnerable overseas stations. Between 1938 and 1944 the total traffic handled by the company increased by 205 per cent.   19/7/1945

Oldest Show Revived After War Years

Oldest show of its kind in the county (it was founded in 1834), and in pre-war days one of the premier Cornish attractions, Stithians Agricultural Association's exhibition of horses, cattle, horticulture, domestic produce, needlework and handicrafts was successfully revived on Monday (Feast Monday) after a lapse of six years and gives every indication of a further long and prosperous career. Attendance was estimated at well over 2,000.   19/7/1945

Death Of "The Cornish Nightingale"

A Cornish singer who won herself a great reputation in her own country, the British Empire and America, Dame Fanny Moody, a prima donna of the 1890's and the early years of the present century, died at her Irish house, The Hermitage, Dundrum, County Dublin, on Saturday, at the age of 78. For years she was known as "The Cornish Nightingale", and to her talents as a singer she added those of an actress, while no one who knew her was ever likely to forget her great personal charm.   26/7/1945

1946 Crop Changes

Some reduction in Cornwall's acreage under potatoes will probably be permissible next year in spite of the Government decision that the national potato production must be maintained. Cornwall's present potato acreage is approximately 23,000, compared with 3,500 acres in 1939.   26/7/1945

School To Be Closed

Cornwall Education Committee have posted throughout Camborne-Redruth urban district notices intimating that it is proposed to close Kehelland Primary School. For a considerable time senior children from the area have been attending Camborne (Bassett-road) Senior School.   26/7/1945

Christened On Mulberry Pierhead

An unusual christening took place mid-stream in the Helford River last week. The three-week-old son of Mr. Leonard Salisbury, of Durfan, Mawnan Smith, was christened on the pierhead of the famous Mulberry Dock, brought over from the beaches of Normandy after the invasion. The ship's bell was used for the water, and a scallop shell for sprinkling the baby. The service was attended by men of the Royal Engineers. 26/7/1945

H.T.P. At War – Miniature Aircraft Factory At Truro

From September 1939 until V.E. Day, this factory repaired over 1,000 vehicles from Austin 8 scout cars and jeeps to large 8 ton mobile generating vehicles for searchlights. Many rumours as to the class of work undertaken in their showrooms have been circulating in the area. It can now be disclosed, however, that they have been engaged upon repairs of the Spitfire components: elevators, tailplanes, rudders, flaps, etc. Over 8,000 of these components have been repaired in this miniature aircraft factory. They were also responsible for repairs to the Spitfire on the local aerodromes, men eating and sleeping by the aircraft, until the 'planes were serviceable again. A mobile workshop was made available for their use.   30/7/1945

Dominion Forces Tour

Mr. Alex Gregg, county agricultural organiser, explained the reclamation scheme carried out by Cornwall War Agricultural Executive Committee on National Trust land at North Cliffs, Camborne, to members of the Dominion and Colonial forces who are visiting Cornwall on a week's agricultural course.   2/8/1945

Falmouth U.S. Base

The United States Navy's great advanced amphibious base at Falmouth was decommissioned on Tuesday, when its Commanding Officer, Lt.-Com. Charles l. Ashley, turned over American facilities and equipment to the British naval officer in charge. Ald. W. Reep, on behalf of the Town Council, presented Lt.-Com. Ashley with an album containing the names of the members of the council, and a number of local photographs, as a parting gift, and in appreciation of the good feeling that has existed for 2½ years between the U.S.A. and the people of Falmouth. The Mayor

(Mr. E.E. Howard) presented Lt.-Com. J.V. Keogh, U.S.N., with some articles made from

Australian Comforts Fund Hostel, Great Western Hotel, Newquay. Booking a game – F/L M. J. Cassiday of Adelaide. Left to right – W/O. L. Wright, Melbourne, P/O B. Masters, Adelaide, F/O M. Paff, Sydney, F/O J. Rigby, Sydney, F/O O'Halloran, Bondi, Sydney, F/O J. Ringwood, Adelaide. 1/8/1945

serpentine gathered at Kynance, The Lizard.   2/8/1945

Cornwall's Five Members

St. Ives – Capt. N. A. Beechman – Nat. Lib.
Camborne – Com. P. G. Agnew – Nat. Con.
Penryn-Falmouth – Lt.-Col. E. M. King – Labour
Bodmin – Com. Douglas Marshall – Nat. Con.
N. Cornwall – Mr. T. L. Horabin – Liberal   2/8/1945

Prisoners Of War

The Cornwall Prisoners of War Food Parcel Fund came to an end on June 30th, 1945. Since the inception of this fund in March, 1943, the magnificent sum of £45,544 1s 11d has been raised and forwarded to the Duke of Gloucester's Red Cross and St. John's Fund… Cornwall can be very proud of the fact that since 1943, the cost of the ten-shilling weekly food parcel to all prisoners of war from Cornwall held in enemy hands, in Europe, has been met through this appeal.   9/8/1945

Japan Doomed

"Russia has declared war on Japan," President Truman announced in Washington, yesterday. The President gave no further details… M. Molotov, the Soviet Foreign Commissar, yesterday received the Japanese Ambassador, and made the following declaration: "Taking into consideration Japan's refusal to capitulate, the Allies have

Liskeard Dog Show. Mr. S. Pedler of Tremabe, Dobwalls with 1ˢᵗ Prize winner, Collie, "Alphington Selected".   *4/8/1945*

addressed to the Soviet Government an offer to join in the war against Japanese aggression, thereby shortening the duration of the war, reducing the number of victims, and assisting in the speediest restoration of peace".   9/8/1945

Cricket
Since 1939 Cornwall county cricket team has been out of action, because of the war, and in preparation for a resumption of the Minor Counties' championship competition next season, the county cricket club have set about the task of team rebuilding. The side representing Cornwall against the United Services at Mount Wise, on August Bank Holiday, included several new-comers, who performed promisingly.   9/8/1945

Strong Wind For Regatta
Point and Penpol regatta was opened by Maj. M. Petherik, who commended to the large assembly Point and Penpol Welcome Home Fund, which was to benefit by the proceeds. He said they would be glad to see their friends and relatives home once more from overseas. The number of entries in the sailing and rowing classes was large, and some fine exhibitions of seamanship were witnessed from the quay, which was lent for the occasion by Mr. W.J. Ferris. The course ran from Point Quay a considerable distance down the creek and back again. The wind was blowing rather strongly down the creek, and it was during the tacking upstream that the best performances were seen. 16/8/1945

Famous Mines
Will operations ever be resuscitated at the famous United Mines, Gwennap, which, it is stated, up to the time of their closure had been worked for copper only? This question arose at a meeting of Gwennap Parish Council, on Thursday, when further consideration was given to the suggestion brought forward at a previous meeting that some 500 acres of waste land on United Downs, near Carharrack, might prove suitable for afforestation purposes… In Cornwall it had been proved over and over again that deposits of copper in the more shallow workings were followed by tin lodes underneath, and there was no reason why history should not repeat itself at united, though unwatering would be a big problem.   16/8/1945

The World War Ends
This morning Cornwall enters upon the second day of celebrations marking the surrender of Japan and the end of the World War… Yesterday and today were proclaimed official holidays, and in Cornish towns and villages, in bright sunshine, festivities began… Impressive services were held in the churches and chapels, and church bells pealed out their message of final victory thanksgiving.   16/8/1945

Special Vans For Fish From Cornwall
An experiment was started at Penzance, on Monday, aimed at ensuring that fish shall arrive in London as fresh as it leaves Newlyn and other Cornish fishing ports. Last month members of West Cornwall Fishermen's Council and the Newlyn fish producers met members of the G.W.R. to discuss improvements with regard to new rolling stock for fish-carrying. The Cornishmen suggested that the railway experts might evolve a scheme incorporating the introduction of an electric cooling plant selfcontained on each of, or alternatively on a series of, freight wagons; that they be thermostatically controlled; and if possible a rectifier be included, whereby wagons, on weekends when lying, say, at Penzance or Paddington, could be connected to the mains current to obtain a

continuity of the chilling process. 16/8/1945

First Post-War Car

H. T. P. Motors Ltd., Truro, delivered their first post-war car to a customer on Saturday. It was an Austen 10 saloon de luxe, selling at £310, ex works. Whilst the exterior appearance was similar to the pre-war models, many improvements have been incorporated. There is a remarkable absence of obscure little noises which seem inseparable from the inexpensive model. There is no fuss from the engine or any other part, and there was plenty of comfort. Rather than being below pre-war standard, the new car has a finish which is exceptionally high… H.T.P. Motors Ltd., announce that beside the Austen 10 h.p. saloon, the famous Eight is also available against a Ministry of War Transport permit. The 12 h.p. and the new "16" models are now in production. 16/8/1945

Singers Of Many Nations

Mr. S.C. Warren-Wren, the Camp Commandant, conducted a sing-song at the International Camp at Trill, Par, attended by girls and youths from Poland, France, Belgium, Greece and Holland.
This camp was the first of its kind in Great Briton, was organised as a first step in establishing greater friendship and understanding between the young people of the world. 23/8/1945

Cornish Broadcasts

At 6.30 p.m. this (Thursday) evening, *St. Piran and the Visitation*, a radio play, based on Sir Arthur Quiller-Couch's delightful short story, will be broadcast in the West of England Home Service… Billy Bray, the famous 19th Century Evangelist, is a talk by Claude Berry, tomorrow, at 6.30 p.m. The name of Billy Bray is still a household word in the West, and he is known through the American philosopher, William James' classic book, *Varieties of Religious Experience*, for his unorthodox methods of preaching. 23/8/1945

Joyous Celebrations In Cornwall

Cornwall celebrated in hearty fashion the surrender of Japan, which brought to a close the World War that began in September, 1939. Towns and villages were soon beflagged, and hurried arrangements made for public rejoicing befitting such an historic occasion. In particular the children and the old people were remembered, especially the former. Sports, carnivals, and teas in streets and playing-fields were among the highlights of the rejoicings, and at night the sky was aglow with bonfires, into many of which had been tossed effigies of Japanese leaders. The Flora was danced through the streets of many towns and villages, and Helston's celebrations were marked by the Furry Dance in which hundreds of people participated. 23/8/1945

Warning To Motorists

It was pointed out at Camborne Magistrates Court, on Tuesday, that since March it had been obligatory for motorists to have identification plates on their vehicles properly illuminated during the hours of darkness. When Frederick James Butler, Tehidy Mill Farm, Camborne, was summoned for such an offence, Insp. G. Warne said he understood many motorists had experienced difficulty in obtaining lamps suitable for the purpose. There was now on the market a round type of lamp in fairly good supply which could be adapted to comply with the regulations. As this was the first case of its kind to be brought before the court since the lighting restrictions were removed, the Bench fined Butler 5s. but the Chairman (Mr. J.C. Penberthy) said future offences would be dealt with more severely. 30/8/1945

V.J. Day (Victory over Japan) Party – Castle-street, Bodmin.   *31/8/1945*

Animals Killed By Lightning

During the heavy thunderstorm very early on Tuesday morning, Mr. Edgar Gay, of Tregolls Farm, Stithians, had six valuable dairy bullocks killed. When the herdsman went to bring them to the milking shed, he found one dead in the gateway and the other five huddled together in the field. Mr. Oswald Knuckey, of Tretheague Mill Farm, Stithians, lost a valuable mare and colt, which he found killed at Carn Rocks. The mare was dead on top of the colt's body. Messrs. J. Hosking and Sons, of Lesneague Farm, St. Keverne, had their best horse killed. Also killed was a heifer belonging to Mr. John Bray, of New Barns, St. Keverne.   30/8/1945

Cloudburst At Falmouth

Whilst on the outskirts of Falmouth at about 3.30 on Thursday afternoon, the sun was shining brightly and farmers were busily cutting and carrying corn, in the town of Falmouth itself one of the worst floods was experienced for 60 years. There was a cloudburst, and in a few minutes a seething torrent from the hills carried everything before it. Large cases, boxes, and handcarts were swept down the streets like corks. One of the most seriously affected parts of the town was the low-lying Market Strand. Traffic was completely stopped, the water being several feet in depth. The business premises were flooded, and considerable damage was done to stock. Motor cars parked at the entrance to the Prince of Wales Pier were filled with water… Sewer covers were swept off. People who had gone to shelter on the Pier were marooned… About twenty minutes elapsed before the flood subsided.   6/9/1945

Record-Breaking Pilot

The pilot of the R.A.F. Mosquito, which flew from St. Mawgan, near Newquay, to Torbay, Newfoundland, on Thursday, in seven hours two minutes – the fastest recorded east to west Atlantic crossing – was Wing Commander J.R.H. Merifield, D.S.O., D.F.C. , with bar, and American D.F.C., son of Capt. and Mrs. J.H. Merifield, Southampton, and formerly of Feock. Aged 24, he is the nephew of Miss M. Merifield, of Pill Creek, Feock… The plane in which he crossed the Atlantic on Thursday was on a duty flight and was not seeking records, although it was thought that a fast flight might be accomplished in spite of Atlantic winds and weather that was not too favourable. The distance covered was about 2,300 miles. The aircraft took off from St. Mawgan at 12.45 p.m. B.S.T. The Mosquito, a photographic reconnaissance aircraft of R.A.F. Coastal Command, is believed to have knocked five hours off the best previously recorded east to west crossing of the Atlantic. 13/9/1945

Large Crowds At Two Cornish Air Stations

In commemoration of the Battle of Britain in 1940, many R.A.F. stations were thrown open to the public throughout the country on Saturday, and in Cornwall large crowds visited St. Eval and Predannack. Vehicles of all descriptions passed along the main Helston – Lizard road to Predannack, and many pedestrians also made the journey, and all felt amply rewarded by the intimate knowledge they gained of the great work of the R.A.F. They were able to see the arrival of a squadron of Mosquitos, and a display of rockets from the control tower attracted much attention. Many visited the station's cinema as guests of the station.

As at Predannack so at St. Eval, all members of the station laid themselves out to make the visitors feel at home. Over 1,500 cars made the trip from near and far to St. Eval, and 48 'buses added their quotas to the crowds of visitors. Here also there was an attractive

Wedding with many of the guests and the bridegroom and sometimes the bride as well in uniform. Typical of very many weddings during the war.

Trethowal Welcome Home Carnival. At the head of the procession A.T.S. Stella May Rogers and Gunner Fred Westaway sitting on the car.   *22/9/1945*

and instructive display of pyrotechnics. St. Eval is the only station in the West of England which has fog dispersal plant.   20/9/1945

Sequel To Storm Crash

In September, 1942, an aircraft which had been on an operational flight from Norfolk to Gibraltar, tried to land in Cornwall in a terrific storm and its four occupants were killed. They were the pilot, Tom Farrer, of Toovak, Victoria, Australia; the navigator, John Granger, a Canadian; and the wireless operator and air gunner, John Holloman and Les Waters, of New South Wales, Australia. They were buried at St. Columb, and the Rev. L.V. Jolly, then vicar of St. Eval and now vicar of St. Day, who officiated at the funeral, has received a letter from the mother of the pilot. She had just heard from an airman friend of her late son, who had been to see the grave, of which he had taken a photograph. He had also informed her that the funeral service was conducted by Mr. Jolly, to whom she writes that the young pilot was one of her two children… They are a British family, and when shipping conditions permit they hope to pay a visit to Cornwall.   20/9/1945

Cornish War –Time Excavations

Mr. C.K. Croft Andrew, a member of the Council for British Archaeology, lectured at Plymouth Athenaeum, on Thursday, on "Recent archaeological work in Cornwall". Mr. Jas. Palmer, president of the Athenaeum, pointed out that Mr. Croft Andrew, throughout the war, had been vigorously engaged in protecting our archaeological treasures on the sites excavated for the massive new aerodromes in Cornwall. Many recalled the particular pride and gratification the success of his assistance in opposition to Bodmin Moor becoming a permanent target area. *There then follows a lengthy article listing each site of interest.* 27/9/1945

Bomber Crash

The interment took place, at Kenwyn, on Saturday, following the funeral service at St. George's Church, Truro, of L.A.C. William Roy Nicholls (Nick), aged 22, younger son of Mr. and Mrs. W.C.O. Nicholls, of "Rosewyn", Rosewin-row, Truro, who was among the twelve airmen killed, when a Halifax bomber crashed ten miles from Launceston, on Friday… Flying-Officer Snow represented the officer commanding Portreath Air Station, and commanded a detachment of airmen who acted as bearers. A Union Jack covered the coffin. 27/9/1945

Cornish Flowers Cheered Wounded In Hospital

Quantities of flowers produced by commercial growers in Cornwall have been given under "silent" social service to cheer and comfort thousands of wounded sailors, soldiers, and airmen in Service hospitals in the Home Counties and the Midlands. The scheme, known as "Fosh" (signifying "Flowers for our Service hospitals") was inaugurated on June 29th, 1944, just after D-Day, when wounded men from the Normandy beaches were returning to England. Boxes of cut flowers, pot plants and market bunches of flowers have been given regularly by growers, wholesale florists and retailers, and as a result from 30 to 60 market packages have been despatched weekly to 42 Service hospitals. Every hospital has received a supply of flowers fortnightly, consignments varying from one to three boxes, according to the number of Service patients. 4/10/1945

Knell Of East Pool Sounded Death

The death knell of east Pool and Agar Mine, as a separate undertaking, has been sounded. The scheme submitted to the Ministry of Fuel and Power for the future of the property in the form of a development programme by diamond drilling has not been approved. This decision has caused surprise as well as regret, for it is believed that the committee of mining experts who thoroughly investigated the proposition reported favourably on it. 4/10/1945

Running Again – Travelling Post Offices To The West

The Travelling Post Offices are running again on the G.W.R. They began their nightly run again a week ago, after an absence of over five years. They carried the Royal Mail between Paddington and the West of England and South Wales. For six nights a week these trains, with sorting staffs working at top speed over the 325 miles' journey, leave Paddington at 10.10 p.m. and Penzance at 6.40 p.m… The first train, which was drawn by one of the "Castle" class locomotive – greyhounds of the G.W.R. track – consisted of a Travelling Post Office unit of five coaches specially constructed at the G.W.R. Swindon Works, and several large vans carrying bags of mail destined for places en route. The coaches forming the Travelling Post Office unit are fitted with benches, pigeon-holes, and boxes to enable mail to be sorted during the journey. 8/10/1945

Impressive Exhibition By St. Ives Artists

The autumn exhibition of St. Ives Society of Art was opened at their new gallery, Porthmeor-square, on Saturday, by Lady du Maurier, of Fowey, who was introduced to the large gathering by Mr. Leonard J. Fuller (chairman of the society). This was a time, said Mr. Fuller, of great encouragement to all artists to get to work and again make that world we all so desired. Artists had every chance of co-operating to bring that ray of light which was so badly needed.   18/10/1945

'Bus Passenger Cuts in South – West

The war-time relaxation of the rule limiting the number of standing passengers in 'buses in the South-Western Region has been removed, and from Sunday (October 14th) no more than eight people will be allowed to stand except during specified "rush hours". *These times were between 5 a.m. and 9.30 a.m., 11.30 a.m. and 2.30 p.m., on all week days, and 4.30 p.m. to 7 p.m. Monday to Friday.*   18/10/1945

First In Cornwall?

Believed to be the first of its kind in Cornwall, a club for men and women over 60 years of age, was inaugurated at Camborne Community Centre, on Tuesday, the large room being filled. At the outset the club will meet on Tuesday afternoons, and, if it is found necessary, a second afternoon will be added. In addition to the large room for a mixed club, there will be separate club rooms upstairs for men and women, who will be able to do just what ever they feel inclined: engage in general conversation , reading, playing draughts, and other games, etc. Refreshments will be served, and there will also be occasional musical and other programmes.   25/10/1945

Bodrugan's Leap For The Nation

Mrs. Guy Campbell has presented to the National Trust a strip of land at the tip of Bodrugan's leap, half-way between Mevagissey and the Dodman, on the Cornish coast. This striking headland, immediately to the south of Chapel Point, will be a notable addition to the trust's possessions in Cornwall, with fine views towards their Dodman properties. According to tradition, the name dates back to the time of Henry V11, when Sir Henry Trenowth, of Bodrugan, a partisan of Richard III, was closely persued by Sir Richard Edgcumbe. Trenowth gained the summit of the rock, leaped into the sea, and escaped to France in a waiting boat. Mrs. Campbell's gift, made in memory of her English husband, is an expression of the love of an American-born woman for the land of her adoption.   25/10/1945

> You can keep your flying fishes
> And your road to Mandalay,
> Your dawns that come too early, and
> Your nights in old Cathay.
> I'm a simple-hearted soldier
> With a single simple need;
> I'd swop the whole darned Orient for
> An English book to read.

Books and magazines are needed more than ever by our Forces overseas now that hostilities have ended. Keep up the supply! Go over your bookshelves regularly and turn out every book you can spare. Hand them over to any post-office counter without wrapping, stamps or label. Just say: Books for the Forces.
Issued by the Ministry of Information.   29/10/1945

Starved For Labour

"Farms are starving for labour", declared Mr. T.D. Dale, at a well attended meeting of

Falmouth Farmers' Union, on Saturday. Moving that the branch should urge that farm-workers now in H.M. Forces should be given every consideration for an early release, Mr. Dale said that labour was a burning question. On some farms, because of the shortage, crops were not being dealt with to the best advantage. It was resolved that county head-quarters be assured of the support of the branch in any steps taken to speed up the release of agricultural workers.   1/11/1945

Germany's Surrender – Cornishmen Help To Erect Memorial

Four Cornishmen associated with the quarrying industry working in the Hartz Mountains, in Central Germany, have quarried 12 tons of granite with which Royal Engineers have fashioned a memorial to mark the spot on the rolling Luneburg Heath, where the German forces in the North-West surrendered to Field-Marshal Montgomery. The names of the Cornishmen are:- Lieut. R.D. McLeod, of Penryn, Lce. Sergt. E.J. Gilbert, Erisey-terrace, Falmouth, Lce. Sergt. W.R. Gluyas, Ivy House, Penstruthal, Redruth, and Sapper S.R. Odgers, Albert-cottages, Falmouth. The memorial will bear the small bronze shield with crossed swords of the 21st Army group, and a copper plaque inscribed: "Here, at 1830 hours on May 4th, 1945, a delegation from the German High Command surrendered unconditionally to Field Marshal Montgomery all land, sea, and air forces in North-West Germany, Denmark, and Holland, and signed a declaration to that effect".   1/11/1945

German Prisoner of War Camp. Toys made by Karl Reister and Wolfgang Petersen for children at the Bristol Hospitals.   *Late 1945*

Helston Loss – The Downs Taken For Air Station

Although residents of the town had known of the matter for some time, it was not until the annual meeting of Helston cricket Club, on Saturday, that any public statement had been made regarding the loss to the borough of the large tract of land known as Helston Downs, where from time immemorial successive generations of Helstonians had assembled for games and other forms of recreation. The whole of the land has been included in the area absorbed in the laying out of the Fleet Air Arm Station. The cricket club's playing pitch had for many years been on the Downs.   1/11/1945

Water On Farms

In his annual report as Medical Officer for West Penwith rural district, Dr. R.H. Hadfield records that, due to lack of water supply on the majority of farms in the district, it was difficult to ensure the proper cleansing of cow sheds. When the proposed comprehensive scheme materialised it would go a long way towards solving the problem of a sufficient supply of pure water to the majority of farms in the area. Sites for the erection of approximately 212 houses in various parts of the area had been selected, and proposals submitted to the Ministry concerned. It was hoped in the next financial year to put into operation a scheme for the collection of household refuse throughout the area by the council's own vehicles.   1/11/1945

No Royal Cornwall Show Until 1947

The decision to hold the Royal Cornwall Show next year will not be carried out. The council of the association were anxious to do so, but it became obvious that nothing would be possible beyond a small one-day show, and the Ministry of Agriculture made it clear that the labour shortage, the demand for timber for housing, food shortage and other factors made it very undesirable to hold large scale agricultural shows next year. The council hope that the invitation from Truro will stand for 1947, so that a show more in keeping with the Royal Cornwall may be possible.   8/11/1945

Large Pears

Sir – I recently picked three pears in my garden of an aggregate weight of 3¾ lbs., the heaviest being 21 ounces, the others 20 and 19 ounces respectively.
                    Yours truly, E. Lemin. Station-road, Pool, Carn Brea.   15/11/1945

Famous Singer's Visit

Unprecedented scenes were witnessed at Gulval Church, near Penzance, on Sunday evening, when 800 people packed themselves into a little church that has a capacity of some 500 people at the outside. Two hours before the service began there were several people already sitting in the nave. Many heard the service from the porch or from the churchyard. The great attraction, in addition to the fact that it was Feast Sunday, was the visit of Madam Gladys Harris, the Cornish contralto, who sang "He Shall Feed His Flock" (Messiah), "Unmindful of the Roses", "Trees", and "Absent". She was accompanied by Mr. E. Tregarthan at the organ.   15/11/1945

Successful Small Holder

Mr. R.J. Luscombe, of The Vale, Colan, is kept fully employed on a holding of 9½ acres. Three acres are ploughed, and on the remaining 6½ acres ten cattle are kept all the year round. He has six dairy cows which are milked three times daily. From September 30th, 1944 to September 30th, 1945, 5,941 gallons of milk were sold. Before taking the holding

Bodmin Hospital Pound Day. *1/12/1945*

Mr. Luscombe was a farm worker. 22/11/1945

£1,785 For Six Chairs

High prices were paid at Christie's on Thursday, for some fine pieces of old English furniture from various sources. Viscount Clifden sent from Lanhydrock, near Bodmin, six George 1st. walnut arm chairs, the arm supports and cabriole legs carved with foliage and lion's claw feet, the seats and backs covered with flowered pink silk brocade, bordered with brass bosses. These changed hands for £1,785. They were probably made for Edward, Lord Harley, son of the Earl of Oxford and Mortimer, Lord High Treasurer to Queen Anne. 22/11/1945

Headstone Used As Hearth Stone

When an old floor at the residence of Mrs. Trenoweth, Carnon Mine, Devoran, was taken up, it was discovered that the slate hearth stone was an old headstone. It measured 31 in. by 17 in., with engravings on the top and one side. The letters, which were carved out very clearly, were of good workmanship, but one side of the stone had been reduced, with a portion of each line of words missing. The stone apparently commemorates the death of Mary, the wife of William (the surname is missing), of the Devonshire town of Barnstaple, who died in 1760. 22/11/1945

"Gross Disfigurement"

Sir – During the past few weeks, the beauty of one of the finest creeks of the Fal – Restronguet – has been ruined for many of the people living on its shores by the dumping of five submarines. It would be hard to picture anything more hideous than a submarine left high, if not dry. How long are they to remain here? One has visions of derelict submarines lying about the coast between the two wars. Their value as scrap appears to be small. Is it not illogical to enforce building restriction in order to preserve the beauty of the Cornish coast and then to allow this gross disfigurement of a very lovely part of the county?   Yours faithfully,

L. Harper, Trolver Croft, Feock, near Truro.   6/12/1945

German Prisoners

The sudden withdrawal of German prisoner-of-war labour from farms in Mid – Cornwall area last week alarmed farmers, who expressed a fear that they would be unable to carry out the instructions of the Cornwall War Agricultural Executive Committee in regard to production… The removal of German prisoner-of-war Labour does not apply in other parts of Cornwall, stated Mr. Wilson, as all the other camps were specifically allocated for agricultural work. Italian prisoners of war will shortly be repatriated in batches, according to age groups, and it is likely that the first batch will leave Cornwall before Christmas… At present there are about 1,200 Italian prisoners in the county, and 760 Germans (including the 309 at Consol Mine).   6/12/1945

Food Fact – Our Christmas Rations

There will be special rations of sugar, butter and margarine, meat, and sweets. Vegetarians will be able to get extra cheese instead of meat.
Sugar – The sugar coupon No. 22 will be worth 1½ lb. sugar, instead of ½ lb. normal ration.

Mr. Sam Quintrell, aged 90, Captain of the Tower of St. Columb Parish Church.   *7/12/1945*

Butter and Margarine – The fats coupon No. 22 will be worth 12 oz. butter and margarine (not more than 6 oz. butter), and 2 oz. cooking fats (instead of the normal ration of 6 oz. butter and margarine, and 2 oz. cooking fats.) This coupon can be used any time during the four-week period No. 6 (Dec. 9th – Jan. 5th).

Meat – Increased from 1s. 2d. to 2s. (7d. to 1s. for children), Ration Book 1 holders. *For ration book holders in other groups different amounts.* For Vegetarians, special cheese rations will be worth 18 oz.

Chocolates and Sweets – an extra 4 oz. of chocolate and sweets.   10/12/1945

Moorland Experiment

Seven selected spots on Bodmin Moor are to be specially treated as an experiment with a view to improving the grazing value of the moorland, and in this project Cornwall Commoners' Association, at Bolventor, on Saturday, decided to co-operate with the County War Agricultural Committee. It was agreed that expenses should be met by a pro rata deduction from the hill cattle and sheep subsidence paid to Commoners in respect of animals grazed on the open moorland. Mr. Alex Gregg (county agricultural organiser) said that the proposition was that they should take plots of, say, seven acres and divide them into acre portions. They wanted the Commoners to "swale" (burn off) half of the plots, the other half to remain "unswaled". On one acre it was intended to put 10 tons of Harlyn Bay or Mother Ivy sand – the best in Cornwall. Then there would be an acre on which they would do nothing – a kind of control. The next acre they were going the "disc" or otherwise treat to allow the sand to get further down into the soil. The fourth acre would be a control, and on the fifth it was intended to place 10 tons of sand and also phosphate. Then there would be another control, and the last plot would be sanded and phosphated and seed cleanings would be used similar to what had been done in the Welsh hill grazings.   13/12/1945

Food Stocks Low

The Isles of Scilly were almost completely cut off from the mainland during last week. This was due to bad weather and the engine trouble to the motor vessel Empire Jonquil, which had been in service while the R.M.S. Scillonian was undergoing her annual survey. Food supplies in the islands ran very low, and there was very little beer. On Thursday morning a specially chartered 'plane of the Great Western and Southern Air Lines arrived with overdue letters and parcels.   13/12/1945

First Since 1938

Truro Fat Stock Society's first post-war exhibition was held in the City Hall, yesterday, when Messrs. F.C. Trewin and Sons, Ruan Minor, with a fine Aberdeen Angus bullock, secured the society's championship prize for best beast in the show and also The West Briton Challenge Cup. Mr. Spencer Jacka, Helston, obtained reserve champion with a Devon bullock. Mr. Jacka has won a champion and two reserve champions with this breed at the three Cornish fat stock shows.   13/12/1945

Killagorden Sold

The free-hold county residence, Killagorden, in the Idless Valley, Truro, the residence of the late Mr. and Mrs. C.M. Knowles, was sold by auction yesterday at Truro by Mr. W.H. Cornish, to Mr. R.H. Dean, of Hatchmans, Beacon-road, Seaford, Sussex, for £4,500. Bidding started at £3,000. Mr. F.R.L. Frank was the solicitor.   13/12/1945

Opening Of New Electric Organ Blower

Mr. William Jenkin, of Carnkie, in spite of his 86 years, continues to take an active interest in Carnkie Wesley Church, of which he is the oldest member. Mr. Jenkin took a foremost part in the scheme which led, in 1936 to the installation in the church of a new two-manual pipe organ, and in the church on Saturday he formally switched on the power to operate the new electric blower, provided at a cost of £85 10s., the whole of which had been raised before Saturday.   20/12/1945

Oates Hotel, Redruth

'Phone 30   Open to non-residents for
Lunches 3/-   Teas 1/6   Dinners 3/6   Book your table early.
Christmas Day Dinner, 5/- at 7.30p.m.   Boxing Day, Children's Tea, 2/6
Send your Kiddies to enjoy the fun.
Farmers' Lunches every Friday, 2/6   20/12/1945

Toys From Australia

Miss L.A. Eustice (headmistress of Roskear Infants' School, Camborne) has received four parcels of beautiful toys made by Mrs. E. O'Brien, View-street, Mentone, Melbourne, Australia, and her daughter, for the children of the school. Before she went to Australia, many years ago, Mrs. O'Brien lived at Beacon, Camborne, and was associated with Treslothan Church. The children were presented with these and other gifts at the annual Christmas party in the school yesterday, by Mrs. E.A. Cock (a manager). Tea was served, and another attraction was the performance of a Nativity play by scholars. 27/12/1945

Peace-Time Christmas Once More

The first peace – time Christmas for seven years was a happy festival in Cornwall, although many of its appurtenances did not come up to popular expectation. The church bells, with their message of "Peace on earth, goodwill to men," heralded a day of bright sunshine in many parts of the county, with an invigorating breeze. In thousands of Cornish homes the difficulties of assembling the fare and providing for the children's stockings were soon forgotten in seeing the vacant chairs once more filled, or in the knowledge that the boys still serving were not in the midst of the thunder of battle, as so many of them were a year ago. There were few outdoor attractions, and most people made merry at their own fireside.   27/12/1945

1946

More Feeding – Stuffs To Be Imported

More important feeding–stuffs will be available during 1946 – 7 livestock rationing period than during the current twelve months, it is officially stated. No information is yet available as to the extent of the increase or the particular feeding concentrates that will be affected, but it is quite definite that the increases will not be dependent upon the American loan. The United States are not the main source of supply. "Cornish farmers can look forward to a further recovery in their livestock populations".   3/1/1946

Bananas arriving at Bodmin station. The three little boys were hoping for a hand out!   *3/1/1946*

Game With New Zealanders

Application for stand tickets (7/6 each) for the Rugby football match, combined Devon and Cornwall XV v New Zealand Touring Team (Army), at Torquay, on February 16th, should be made not later than January 26th, to Mr. W.J. Robbins, Taquah House, Camborne, stamped addressed envelope with remittance to accompany each request.   3/1/1946

New Year Peal

A peal on the bells of Truro Cathedral heralded the New Year, and at the railway station whistles were blown.   3/1/1946

"999" Emergency Call

The Post Office introduced the "999" scheme for emergency calls on Tuesday, at Truro. The new scheme enables the caller, whether from a private telephone or a public call office, by dialling "999" instead of "0", to secure the special attention of the operator for calls to the Fire, Police or Ambulance Service on occasions of emergency. For this purpose, special equipment has been installed at the Truro Exchange so that, when "999" is dialled, an emergency lamp and loud buzzer will indicate to the operator that the call is specially urgent. The telephone numbers of the Fire, Police and Ambulance Authorities are prominently displayed for the information of the operators, and connection with these authorities will be secured by simple asking the exchange operator for "Fire!", "Police!", or "Ambulance!", as the case may be. It cannot be too strongly emphasised that the number "999" should be dialled only when the Fire, Police or Ambulance Service is needed in circumstances of real urgency, and never for any other purpose whatsoever. 3/1/1946

At The King's Stables

At the invitation of the Crown Equerry, Mr. and Mrs. W.A. Eddy, Treloweth Manor, St. Erth, their son (Master Michael Eddy), and three daughters (the Misses Nancy, Jill, and Rachael Eddy), paid a visit to the King's Stables at the Royal Mews, Buckingham Palace, yesterday, at the first public inspection since before the war.

Mr. Eddy's children are well-known riders of horses at Cornish agricultural shows. Last year they secured no fewer than 189 awards, including many beautiful silver trophies. 3/1/1946

The Fordson Plough

is doing such an excellent job of work wherever in use that we are quite prepared for you to try one on your own farm, in your own conditions, without any obligation whatsoever. Book early, please!

2 – furrow General Purpose, £53-10-0   3-furrow General Purpose, £64-10-0

Truro Garages Ltd., Truro. 'Phone 2353.   3/1/1946

Wassailing

Wassailing, which has taken place at Bodmin almost without a break on Old Christmas Day for 150 years, was a feature of the week-end at the county town, when £8 was raised for aged poor. Among the wassailers was Mr. John Clemo, of Plymouth, whose great-grandfather used to take part in the old custom, and who had himself maintained the tradition for 63 years.   10/1/1946

Orange Juice Scheme Is Permanent

Mr. H. Goodman presided at Lostwithiel Food Control Committee, on Friday, when Mr. S.C. Brown was re-elected chairman and Mr. H. Goodman, vice-chairman. The Food Executive Officer, Mr. F.J. Jeffery, read a letter from Sir Ben Smith (Minister of Food), regarding the necessity of continuing the rationing scheme for a time, and also pointing out that the orange juice vitamin scheme for children was permanent. It was stated that the school canteen was very satisfactory, and of great benefit. Shopkeepers complained of the great wastage in the recent issue of oranges, and Mr. Jeffery said the matter was being investigated. 10/1/1946

Milk Rationing
No date for the end of milk rationing could be given by Mr. Tom Williams, Minister of Agriculture, when questioned at a luncheon at the Women's Press Club, in London, yesterday. "If the present demand for milk persists and we continue to provide for priority consumers, I am afraid rationing will remain for a long time," he said. 10/1/1946

Hounds Meet At Penzance
For the first time in the history of Penzance the Western Foxhounds met in the borough itself on Friday, following the hunt ball at the Winter Garden the previous evening. The meet, which attracted many hundreds of the general public, was held in the fore-court of the Municipal Buildings. The Mayor (Ald. Robert Thomas) attended and provided the riders, of whom there were some 50, with a stirrup cup before they moved away in pouring rain in the direction of Tremethick. Mr. Leslie Oats, the master, was present, with Mrs. Oats as whipper-in. There were 18 couple of hounds out. 17/1/1946

Ford Anglia
The Ford 8 h.p. Anglia, the only car to have been designed in the war years, has ample luggage accommodation, full seating for four persons, and engine performance is out-standing. Smoothness of running has been introduced through larger shock absorbers being used, and improvement in lighting is beyond the highest hopes. This car, upholstered in imitation hide, is the lowest priced eight horse-powered in the market. It is on view at Truro Garages, Ltd., Lemon Quay. 17/1/1946

Beach Minefields
The operation of clearing two minefields on the beach at Perranporth is to be carried out by military experts during the next three or four months. The position will require careful handling, as the location of the mines has been rendered more difficult because the sand dunes have shifted since the mines were laid in the early days of the war. It is believed that some of the mines are now buried from 15 to 20 feet deep. Bulldozers will be used to remove the banks of sand around the dunes, and the minefields will be tackled by powerful water-jets washing away the sand which covers them. 17/1/1946

"Something To Think About," said Mrs. Tremayne
"When electricity bill arrived I just used to grumble and get the thing paid. But this time the girl in the Service Centre let me see our account in her ledger – I could hardly believe my eyes. In 1928 we paid £18 14s 4d for 463 units – now we're getting 5,030 units for £21 10s 7d – less than £3 extra. I know the more you use the less it costs – and it's saved me a good deal of effort. Electricity does make a difference in running a home." (These are authentic cases from the Group's Records)
Cornwall Electric Power Co., Central Office, Carn Brea. Telephone 2201/4. 21/1/1946

Dog Racing Track
Sir – It is with grave concern we hear of the proposed greyhound racing track in Camborne – Redruth district. This is an industrial area – too often a distressed area. We

view with alarm this menace to our young people, with its temptation to gambling and attendant vices. The intending disaster is a blot on the fair face of Cornwall, whose men and women, by honest toil and sweat, have brought fame and honour to their county. Why build huts for hounds when houses are such a dire necessity to our returning ex-Servicemen? What is the insidious motive at the bottom of this venture? Not to benefit the district. Gamblers are not philanthropists. Let the women of every church, organisation, and community rise and protest against this modern canker of society with which we are threatened. Yours Truly, A. L. Bath.

Coronation-road, Redruth.   24/1/1946

There followed a great deal of articles, letters etc. over many months but in the end the greyhound racing track was not built.

One He Missed

A mine, which subsequently proved to be British, was observed by The Lizard Coast-guards on Wednesday, close inshore near Polpeor, where The Lizard lifeboat is stationed. Mr. R. Phillips and others tried to secure the mine, but were unsuccessful. Mr. and Mrs. Arthur Matthews had to leave their bungalow on the cliffs overlooking the cove. Mr. Matthews, who has recently been demobilised from the Navy, spent nearly six years in mine-sweepers. Eventually the mine was washed ashore and a mine disposal squad, under Lieut. Pratt, R.N.R., of H.M.S. Defiant, rendered it harmless.   24/1/1946

Houses From China Clay Sand

One of the "unit" specimen prefabricated houses built at Bugle for the Central Cornwall Concrete Co., of concrete blocks made from material obtained from the huge dumps of china clay residue, which are a feature of the mid-Cornwall countryside. Made in the company's works, the blocks are easily transportable and assembled on building sites, and it is estimated that the costs would be in the region of 21s. 6p. per foot super. With the exception of the wood, all materials are available locally.   7/2/1946

Gales And Storms

Gales and storms during the past week are estimated to have cost flower growers in the Scilly Isles some £12,000… Violets have suffered …wallflowers are firmer, and so, too, are marigolds. Prices of pittosporum have recovered… Primroses are now arriving regularly, and make 6d a bunch… Prices of snowdrops… have slumped with an increase in supply… The supply situation had become acute in the islands until Tuesday. In the morning the Great Western and Southern Air Lines 'plane, piloted by Capt. Hearne, brought the mail, which was seven days overdue. In the afternoon, at the instigation of the local food Office and Ministry of Food, who specially chartered the 'plane, the long overdue week's supply of beef arrived. Half an hour later the Admiralty barge brought sausages and a general supply of rationed goods.   7/2/1946

Illegitimacy

Sir – In your issue of January 24th, observations by the County Medical Officer showed clearly that Camborne-Redruth had an illegitimate birth-rate very much lower than some parts of the county and thus countered the suggestion advanced in your correspondence columns by a correspondent that Camborne-Redruth had the highest rate in the county. It may not be generally realised that various maternity institutions in Camborne-Redruth cater largely for areas outside the town. Of 581 births in the Redruth registration area in 1941, 228 were of families resident outside the urban district. The total number of illegitimate children born in the urban district that year was 44; yet only 25 of these had local mothers...

More than once in responsible quarters I have heard references to the supposed excessive immorality in Cambore-Redruth. I have lived here 25 years and the statistics I have quoted bear out my own impression that our town is one of the cleanest towns in the country from a moral standpoint.

Yours truly, F.H. Hayman. 3, West Park, Redruth.   7/2/1946

Cooked Over 23,000 Dinners

Mrs. Lilian Brown has completed her forth year of service as cook at St. Michael Penkivil canteen. She has been neither absent nor late, and in stormy weather. Mrs. Brown and the headmistress and the assistant teacher have rowed themselves across the River Fal from Malpas. In the performance of her duties Mrs. Brown has cooked 23,261 dinners of three courses, walked 630 miles carrying an average weight of 231 lbs. in water, vegetables, or coal, and climbed a quarter million steps.   7/2/1946

£650 House At St. Ives

The first of the permanent houses *has been* erected by direct labour by St. Ives Town Council, at an approximate cost of £650.   14/2/1946

New Treatment For Silicosis

Research into the treatment of silicosis and methods to prevent its onset has been proceeding in the mining areas all over the world for many years. A method using finely-powered aluminium has been developed in Canada and the workers there claim a great measure of success for it... This claim is so important that the Medical Research Council are sending a staff of research workers to Cornwall in order to arrange for the application of preventive measures in Geevor and South Crofty Mines. The method consists of nothing more than spraying a very small quantity of aluminium dust into the changing room. This dust being inhaled, becomes mixed with the dust of the mine workings and is stated to neutralise the silica particles which cause the disease... Silicosis is of such a nature that it cannot actually be cured.   14/2/1946

Roman Coin Found At Wadebridge

While crossing the bridge at Wadebridge on his way to school, Robert Moss picked up a Roman coin, a denarius of Probus, who was Emperor from 276 to 283 A.D. "Does this find indicate the presence of a hoard near-by?" asks Robert's headmaster, Mr. T. Oates, who adds, such hoards have been found – two or three in West Cornwall, at Caerhays and Mulfra Hill – presumably in connection with the revival of tin-streaming from A.D. 250-340, when the Roman supplies in North Spain began to fail. A find of this period was also made in connection with "tinning" at Carnanton, in Mawgan-in-Pydar, the only one to my knowledge of the date and contex east of Truro. Did this particular coin drop off one of the earth lorries that cross the bridge?

Has any earth been transported from "down in Cornwall" to a northern destination? Such coins are rarely found singly, and their having been found does not mean that any Roman, as such, was ever here; the workings were under British supervision as far as is known.   14/2/1946

Correspodence – Food

Sir – We have been told our bread may be a little darker owing to 85 per cent extraction instead of 80 per cent, but this will give greater nutrition from the bread we eat. As a result of this greater extraction, less offal will be available for feeding animals, particularly pigs, with the consequent loss of bacon. Need there be a shortage of food for pigs? Why not reduce by 50 per cent the barley allocated to producing intoxicating drinks, which are responsible for an appalling amount of misery, many of the accidents on the roads, and an expenditure of some £500,000,000 annually. For the present and in the future bacon is better than beer.

F.W. Bennetts. 2, West Park, Redruth. 14/2/1946

Stranded Ship

There was a sequel at West Kerrier Sessions yesterday to the stranding of the motor ship Fauvette at Trebarwith Beach, St. Keverne, on Sunday, February 4th. Five men, Melville James Nicholls, 6, Coronation-cottages, St. Keverne; John Treloar, 7, Coronation-cottages; John Alan Williams, Porthoustock; Jim Lawrence, Trewillis, St. Keverne; and Fredrick Sidwell, Trevalsoe, St. Keverne, pleaded guilty to being in unlawful possession of goods from the ship of a total value of £10. The value of the goods taken by the men was:- Nicholls, £5 19s. 3½d.; Treloar, £3 10s.; Williams 10½d.; Lawrence, 5s.; Sidwell, 4s. 10d..

Supt. T. Morcumb stated that the ship was bound from Malta to Falmouth with a cargo of ammunition and Naval stores. The crew left the ship at low tide, at 10.30 a.m., and were accommodated in St. Keverne district. He realised that the smuggling instinct was still in existence in Cornwall, but that case was something more than that. The ship was not wrecked but simply stranded, and the men went aboard, commenced to ransack the boat and to carry away goods...

The Chairman, (Mr. J.H. Ould) said... The position of Lawrence was particularly serious in that there was a sense in which he had a considerable amount of responsibility as being left in charge. Lawrence would be fined £5, Treloar £3, Williams 10s., and Sidwell 10s. Each defendant would also have to pay 3s 6d. expenses... The Bench ordered the articles to be restored to the ship, which it is hoped to refloat within the next few days. 14/2/1946

Split Willow Shortage

The President of the Board of Trade was asked in the House of Commons on Monday... For an immediate action to increase supplies of split willow and hazel hoops for lobster and crabpotmaking. 14/2/1946

Had To Pick Sticks

An acute shortage of coal in the parish was reported to Gwennap Parish Council on Thursday, and the Clerk... was instructed to send a telegram to the Regional Officer, at Bristol, ... asking that supplies should be made immediately available. ... Mr. Allen said people in Gwennap were having to pick sticks to cook their meals, and Mr. R. Jory said a parishioner had told him that for eight weeks she had had to take her washing to Falmouth because she had no coal. 21/2/1946

Presumed Killed

Pte. C. Evans, D.C.L.I., fourth son of Mr. and Mrs. W.J. Evans, Scorrier-street, St. Day, who has been missing since November 4th, 1944, is now presumed to have lost his life while attempting to escape from Italy across the Alps into France, while a prisoner of war. Pte. Evans, with a party of other soldiers and Partisans, left Borgiallo, in Italy, on November 4th, in an attempt to cross the frontier, but had the misfortune to encounter bad weather and snowstorms, and as far as can be ascertained, only one British soldier survived. Pte. Evans,

Threshing at Cardinham Downs, Bodmin Moor.   *1/3/1946*

who was a regular soldier, had served 8½ years in India before the outbreak of war. Before joining the Army he was employed at Alma Farm, Highertown, Truro.   28/2/1946

Tablet To Three Young Men Of Mousehole
A tablet to the memory of three young Mousehole men who sailed to Tierra del Fuego on a missionary expedition in 1850 and there died of starvation after suffering great privations, was unveiled at St. Clement's Methodist Church, Mousehole, on Sunday… The lesson was read… by… Corpl. Pentreath Johns, (*a member of the Cornwall Boys' Brigade*) who is directly related to one of the three men whose courage was remembered. The tablet bore the inscription "Keep in proud remembrance John Badcock, John Bryant and John Pearce."   28/2/1946

Famous Jockey At Penzance
Gordon Richards, the famous jockey, and Tom Reece, the billiards champion, have just concluded a ten-days holiday at Penzance. Mr. Dudley Williams (who rode Kelsboro' Jack in the Grand National) and the well-known jockeys, Archie Burns and Ted Gardner, were also members of the party. Golf at Lelant was one of their chief pastimes, and one day they visited Mr. Harry Laity at Bosistow. Mr. Laity's ponies provided mounts for an enjoyable impromptu "race".   28/2/1946

Clearing The Mines
Mine clearance at Perranporth was to have started on Friday, and it was hoped it would have been completed by the end of May. All plant and equipment is being installed with that in view, but owing to some delay with regard to the evacuation of some houses within the danger area, the start has been delayed for probably a week or ten days.

The clearance of beach type mines is being carried out by a composite working party of personal… The mine field consists of two sections with a clear gap of about 90 yards between. One section is about 120 yards long and contains about 40 mines, and the other is about 90 yards long and contains 35 mines. Both sections are situated amongst sand dunes which are wind swept and consequently always changing, so that mines may be buried 10 feet or more, in places, or lying exposed on the surface in other places. 4/3/1946

Dolcoath Siding
In anticipation of increased milk traffic from West Cornwall, Dolcoth Tin Works Siding, Camborne, closed since 1921, was re-opened by G.W.R. on Monday for the dispatched of milk to London. Improvements include drainage and a water supply for washing down milk tanks, a wider road entrance and re-made approach road.   7/3/1946

Peregrine Breeding Stocks In County
The first fully authenticated report of the nightingale in Cornwall has been received from Penzance. This was reported to Cornwall Bird Watching and Preservation Society at its first annual meeting since 1939, at Truro, on Monday. It was also reported that the breeding stock of the peregrine falcon in the county appeared to have been wiped out… The government had authorised the destruction of peregrines … with the result that the breeding stock was wiped out. The destruction of rooks had also been authorised, but ravens had fared well. Choughs had remained at the same low level, but Montagu's Harriers had made a startling and pleasant increase. Fulmars had now begun to breed at more than one station. There had been no evidence of egg-collecting, but there had been a certain number of shooting offences.   7/3/1946

Fishermen And Call-Up
Mr. Douglas Marshall (Con. S.E. Cornwall) asked the Minister of Labour, on Thursday, if in view of the world food situation he would take immediate steps to stop the call-up of fishermen.   7/3/1946

A Big Catch
The largest catch this season by a Newlyn fishing boat was obtained by the longliner Swift (skipper, S. Thomas) on Monday. Although the Swift only put to sea on Monday morning and was back in port within twelve hours, she landed 575 stone of ling, 105 stone of ray, 100 stone of dog-fish and 50 stone of roes and chidlings.   7/3/1946

No Hold Up On New Road
Recently, Mr John Pryor, (secretary), on behalf of Helston Farmers' Union, made representations to the Admiralty…regarding a report that when the new Fleet Air Arm Station being laid down just outside Helston comes into operation, the newly-built Helston-Lizard main road will be closed while 'planes are entering and leaving the aerodrome. Mr. Pryor has heard from Com. Agnew that now the new road has been completed and is in use it will not be necessary for the Admiralty to close it while flying is in progress.   7/3/1946

The Warspite
The training ship, Warspite, which trained thousands of boys for the Royal Navy and Merchant Service, was formally the cruiser Hermione, the keel of which was laid in 1892. The Warspite was adapted for use as a training vessel in 1921, but at the beginning of the war in 1939 the ship was closed, as it was in an evacuation area. The ship was

eventually sold to be broken up for steel scrap. 11/3/1946

Derelict Submarines

The Executive Committee of Cornwall branch of the Council for the Preservation of Rural England...considered a complaint concerning dumping by the Admiralty of derelict submarines between Point and Restronguet, these ugly hulks lie on the foreshore, rusty and grown over with barnacles and make an unsightly and depressing spectacle...

Mr. R.F. Wheatly's report on the Glebe House, St. Columb, stated that a very interesting oriel window existed in a condemmed building near by, which exactly fitted a space in the Glebe House, and he considered that in any demolition scheme it would be desirable to make an effort to preserve this oriel window, in case at some future stage it might be replaced in what was probably its original setting. 14/3/1946

Truro Mayor's Air Trip

The Mayor of Truro (Mr. A.A. Behenna) *made* his first journey by air in a Taylorcraft Auster aircraft, at a demonstration at R.A.F. Portreath. 14/3/1946

Bevin Boys Future

The South-Western Federation of Trades Councils at its annual meeting, on Saturday, passed a resolution from the Cornish Group, asking the T.U.C. to explore the possibilities of abolishing the direction of juniors to the mining industry.

Bevin Boys were young men and boys employed in the mines to relieve the older men to go into the services during the war. 21/3/1946

St. Eval Aerodrome. R.A.F. and Navy Exercises – group of crews round a Lancaster Bomber. 30/3/1946

Rt. Hon. Isaac Foot, Lord Mayor of Plymouth, speaking at Bodmin County School Speech Day.
5/4/1946

Rescuer's Fall

When the rope on which he was being lowered, on Sunday, to rescue a dog which had fallen down a disused mine shaft, broke, Insp. C.J.H. Taylor, of the N.S.P.C.A., Truro, fell 40 feet to the bottom of the shaft, which was covered with thick, soft mud about a foot deep. The mud broke his fall, but he was badly bruised on his right side and back. He is now confined to bed, but is progressing favourably... The dog was hauled to the top in a net cradle...The dog, a small Sealyham mongrel bitch showed not sign of exhaustion. It is now at the inspector's home awaiting an owner.   28/3/1946

Lost 16 Ducks

Mr. J. Pascoe, grocer, Station-road, Pool, lost 16 fully-grown laying ducks on Thursday, while, with Mrs. Pascoe he was at a concert in the village. Mr. Pascoe did not drive the ducks into their house and make it secure before leaving. On his return he found the bodies of six laying about, and ten others were missing... A short time previously Mr. Pascoe had sold three similar ducks for £1 each.   28/3/1946

Cornish Samson

Believed to be one of the strongest men in Great Briton, Dick Williams, known as the Cornish Samson, is prepared to compete or exhibit his feats of strength in any part of the world... He presented an impressive spectacle as he performed his act, stripped to the waist, exposing his brawny chest, measuring 47 inches when expanded, his bicep muscles 17 inches in circumference, and his broad shoulders and back. His first feat was to raise his assistant, Mr. S. Treglown, Penryn, weighing 12 stone 2 lbs., above his head with his right hand, at the same time holding a weight of 70 lbs. above his head with his left hand.   4/4/1946

Heat Wave Spoils Flower Trade
Both condition and prices of Cornish flowers in Covent Garden Market are still under the influence of abnormally warm weather. In spite of the growers' care in packing, over-heating in transport is unavoidable on so long a journey…The market would welcome a return to normal temperatures.   4/4/1946

Diphtheria Incident At Penzance
Welcome news that the incidence of diphtheria in the borough was well on the decline, was given by a councillor, the Rev. C.H.S. Buckly, speaking at a meeting of Penzance Ratepayers' Association, on Friday…There had been a suggestion that visitors should not be encouraged to come to the town this summer, but the danger had now receded and should not be allowed to interfere with the first post-war tourist season. 11/4/1946

Looking Well
Hunt supporters in good numbers turned up at Scorrier House, on Saturday, when, by invitation of the Master, (Mr. Percival Williams) and Mrs. Williams, the Four Burrow Hounds puppy judging took place under ideal weather conditions. Owners paraded their young foxhounds in an informal circle in front of the residence for the inspection of the judges.   11/4/1946

Petrol To Bring Scilly Flowers
Saying that an aeroplane had been chartered to bring flowers from the Scilly Isles at a cost of 100 gallons of petrol, Mr Lewis (Lab., Upton) asked the Minister of Fuel and Power whether, in view of the need for petrol to be used economically, he would take steps to prevent this in future – Mr. Shinwell, in a written answer, says "Allowances of civil aviation fuel are granted to companies operating chartered or taxi flights to provide for limited number of flying hours a month. I do not consider that it would be practicable to restrict the business purposes for which civil aircraft may be chartered for journeys within the limits of the fuel allowances".   11/4/1946

Falmouth Welcome Home
The second dinner and entertainment was given at the Central Services' Club by Falmouth Entertainments Committee to 250 men and women demobbed from the Forces.   18/4/1946

"Dishonest Bill"
A largely-attended meeting of the medical profession in Cornwall was held in Truro, on Sunday, to consider the National Health Service Bill, which is now before Parliament, and to instruct their Representative to the meeting of the British Medical Association, to be held in London in the first week of May. The provisions of the Bill were discussed at some length, and conclusions were reached that the Bill, as it stood, was a dishonest one, and should be resisted as far as possible: and that payment of doctors by even a small basic salary would inevitably lead to whole-time State-salaried medical service.

18/4/1946

Clothing Coupon Offences

An ex-Naval man, Reginald Webber, of 11, West-hill, St. Austell, was fined £7 10s at St Austell, yesterday, for transferring 15 clothing coupons to a person unknown, and 45 coupons to James Charles Reed, 38, South-street, St Austell, who was fined £5 for accepting them. Both Webber and Reed pleaded guilty.   18/4/1946

Parting Gifts

After nearly six years the Royal Netherlands Navy College, at Enys, Penryn, is to be closed on May 1st, and the Navy will leave Cornwall soon afterwards. On Tuesday, officers and men visited Penryn and Falmouth, where presentations were made to the boroughs in commemoration of the Navy's six years stay and in appreciation of the kindness shown by local residents. In a large gathering, at Penryn, were children from the two day schools.

Presenting the Mayor (Mr. H.B. Jennings) with a shield and link to be attached to the mayoral chain of office, Capt. W.F. Von Langeveld said they had seen the town bombed, with grievous loss of life and property, and they had seen the citizens come out undismayed and undented. The people of Penryn had earned their deepest admiration and respect for the way they had done their duty in war-time.   18/4/1946

Record Crowd

Enhancing it's popularity as Cornwall's chief Easter social and sporting event, the Four Burrow Point-to-Point steeplechase, at Penatillie Farm, St Columb, on Monday, attracted a record attendance of 10,000 and there were about 2,000 cars. The long spell of rainless weather had made the ground very dry. The course was on the stiff side, there being a long up-hill climb before the run home. There were no serious accidents, either to horses or riders, although there were several spills at the jumps.   25/4/1946

Milk Rationing May End Next Year

Restriction of the consumer's liberty to buy milk from any dairyman he pleases, and a return to unrestricted competition between milk retailers may be made next year.   25/4/1946

Welcome To G.I. Brides

The New York Cornish Association has written to Helston Old Cornwall Society offering a warm welcome to any G.I. bride who might be going to the U.S.A. in the near future ... It was reported that the revival of the old Hal-an-Tow and the mock Mayor of St. John's, sponsored by the Old Cornwall Society, would take place in the Flora day celebrations, at Helston, on May 8th.

The term "G.I." refers to members of the United States Forces as an initalisation of Government Issue, first used in the First World War, and latterly anything to do with that army. 25/4/1946

Underground Miners' Wages

Speaking at a Labour demonstration at Camborne, on Saturday, Mr. F.H. Hayman (Labour candidate for the division at the last election) said that he had been informed that wages paid to underground miners at South Crofty Mine totalled 11s 6d a shift for a working week of six days, bringing the total for the week to £3 9s., plus a small bonus of 15s a week, payable at the end of a month if the men were sufficiently fortunate to have escaped sickness during the period. There was no occupation in the world more dangerous than that of an underground miner in South Crofty Mine. The Government intended introducing legislation to extend the scope of the fair wages clause in industry, and that would have the result of making provision for the payment of fair wages to workers in every industry. 9/5/1946

Redruth Boxing
The boxing at Redruth, on Thursday evening, promoted by Mr. Chas. Simpson (B.B.B. of C.) was probably one of the best tournaments seen in Cornwall for some time. A crowded house witnessed clean and sustained bouts from beginning to end. Boxers familiar to all Cornish boxing fans, figured prominently, and fully maintained the high standard of west-country boxing. A highlight of the evening was an eight three minute round contest at welterweight between Joe Perks, Lizard, the present West of England title holder, and Percy Barnes, Penzance, who made a name for himself in India in service boxing. Barnes, a southpaw, created a sensation when he put Perks down in the first round for a count of five, but from the third round onwards, Perks was master and carried the fight with ease. 9/5/1946

Coast Road And Houses
Sir – When is the coast road from Porthtowan to Portreath to be opened again to the public? Is anything going to be done with the apparently empty extensive range of buildings in the valley road to Portreath? I believe these were used by the W.A.A.F. during the war. They would be suitable for a holiday camp or even for temporary housing purposes. Enquirer. St Agnes. 9/5/1946

Popular Holywell
All the bungalows and chalets at Holywell requisitioned during the war are now freed, and most of the places are booked up by September and October. The Holywell Bay Hotel is fully booked and has had visitors since Easter. The increase of buses from Newquay and Perranporth brings a great many trippers to the bay. 16/5/1946

County Herb Committee Closes Down
During the war, when it was difficult to obtain supplies of drugs from abroad, Cornwall County Herb Committee was set up, and contributed very substantially and valuable quantities of herb and seaweed for the making of penicillin, digitalin, and other important drugs. The Cornwall committee have decided to close down. They thank all organisations and collectors who helped make the work such a success. It is hoped that the seaweed and rose-hip collectors will continue their activities with the commercial firms concerned. 23/5/1946

Bell-ringers For Over 60 Years
Among the bell-ringers at Ladock Parish Church are three octogenarians, Messrs. R. Gregor (81), W.J. Chapman (81) and S.C. Hooper (87), all of whom have been ringing over 60 years. Messrs. Gregor and Hooper have rung the Christmas peals for the 15th Century church tower for 57 consecutive years. 23/5/1946

Avertisement

have now returned. This means better service for you.

The Railways are getting back to normal.   30/5/1946

Redruth V Day

Arrangements for victory celebrations in Redruth were made at a meeting of local members of the Urban Council on Saturday. It was agreed that, as there would be a large Whitsun fair in the town, it would be inadvisable to organise any out-of-doors function. It was decided to present each old-age pensioner with a gift of two shillings and also to make a monetary presentation and the gift of a commemorative medal to each child. It was reported that local bakers were unable to provide a supply of saffron buns, and in consequence, there will be no tea. The committee of Plain-an-Gwarry Show Society are organising a carnival in the evening on behalf of the Sportsmen's War Memorial Fund and the Town Forces Welcome Home Fund.   30/5/1946

Holidays With Pay

All manual workers employed on electricity supply by the Cornwall Electric Power Company are to have an extra week's holiday with pay each year. A voluntary arrangement between the employers and the employees in the industry will now give the workers two weeks paid holiday as well as six Bank holidays. It will operate as from 1st April, 1946.   30/5/1946

Advertisement

Punch and Judy solicit enquiries for Birthday Parties – Professor Edgar,

63, Commercial-rd., Hayle.   30/5/1946

Penzance Memorial Houses

A pair of houses, to accommodate disabled gunners and their families, in the tangible form of war memorial adopted by Cornwall district of the Royal Artillery Association. The houses, estimated to have cost about £2,500, are to be built at the Parcletta Estate, Penzance, the site and a donation of £100 having been contributed by the Lord-Lieutenant of Cornwall, (Lieut.-Col. E.H. Bolitho), himself a former R.A. officer.   6/6/1946

Meagre Rations

Grave concern was expressed by Mr. E.E. Ayre, Newquay, at St. Columb Farmers' Union, on Thursday, at the small amount of rations allocated to prisoners of war on farm work…On one occasion recently, the prisoners had refused to work unless they could be assured that sufficient rations would be forthcoming.

Question of the use of prisoners of war on V – Day celebrations and Whit Monday was also discussed, and it was felt that payment at the usual rate of 1s. 5½ d., plus holiday rate, 2s 2d, making a total of 3s 7d. per hour for these two days, was absolutely unfair. 6/6/1946

First Of Camborne's Mining Students

Members of Camborne Old Cornwall Society spent an interesting evening, on Saturday, when, by invitation of Mr. and Mrs. D.W. Thomas, they visited Lowenac House and grounds. Mr. Thomas read a paper on "Old Camborne", based on a book of letters dating from 1840. Particularly interesting was an account of the visit to Camborne by a young Egyptian to study mining. Visiting the area through the invitation of Mr. Joseph Vivian, gent., of Reskadinnick, he was the forerunner of all mining students, and it was probably the result of his stay in Camborne that the School of Mines came to be established there.   6/6/1946

Food Waste Protest

Truro Rural Food Committee decided yesterday, Mr. C.H. Hawke (Mitchell) presiding, to draw the attention of the Divisional Food Officer to the waste of food in Cornwall caused by the ploughing in of vegetables and the throwing of fresh fish back into the sea. … Mr. S. Oatey asked why, if herrings could not be sold at 2d., they were not sold at 1½d., rather than returned to the sea. If a loaf of bread was wasted, on the other hand, people were prosecuted. 6/6/1946

Badger Attacks Farmer

While Mr. W.J. Sandow, Chacewater, was walking around his farm, on Sunday, his dogs were attracted to some bushes, and were fiercely attacked by a large badger which afterwards turned on Mr. Sandow. Mr. Sandow called his neighbour, who arrived with his gun, but the badger escaped into a brake. A message was sent to Mr. H.G. Elstone, master of the Elstone beagles, and on Monday, after a long draw, hounds marked their badger in a very deep earth. On Tuesday, Mr. Lawrence, Penhalvean, Redruth, arrived with two terriers which joined the kennel terriers, and after eight hours hard digging, with willing helpers, a very large badger was killed. A lot of damage has been done by badgers among poultry in the district during the past month. 6/6/1946

Redruth Sheepdog

Merriot Matilda, owned by Mr. and Mrs. W. Heyden, of Kaduna Kennels, Redruth, won

Free Rides on a R.A.F. launch on Fowey Victory Day celebrations. 8/6/1946

Ann Todd, the famous film star, at her home at Glendorgal, Porth, Newquay. 9/6/1946

first prize in a special yearling bitch class in a sheepdog section of the English Shetland Sheepdog and Poodle Championship Show in London, on Tuesday. The same dog won third prize in the junior bitch class, and the special owners' bitch class. 6/6/1946

Coast Watchers

At nearly 20 stations in Cornwall coast watchers are needed, and it is hoped that there will be offers to cover all the duties from men who, in a public-spirited way, desire to show gratitude to those who served at sea in the critical years of war. During the war there was little difficulty in obtaining men as Auxiliary Coastguardsmen, because, in addition to the call of public duty, they could be employed regularly at a good living wage. Since the end of the war many lookouts have been closed and others have only value in bad or thick weather, with the consequence that men can be only employed on "part-time" basis. This employment entirely depends on weather conditions, and therefore does not provide a living wage. The actual wage for watchers is 1s. 9d. per hour, with a guaranteed minimum payment of 7s. for a four-hour watch, whether the whole watch is kept or not. 20/6/1946

Manufacture Of Dresses

Jaquemand Ltd., dress manufacturers, London, who for several years have had a branch works at Bideford, are to start operations at Redruth… *They* have acquired the empty building in Green-lane, formerly the Liberal Club, and it is being adapted for the installation of machinery. If the project succeeds, this will be a temporary headquarters only. A site for a factory has already been purchased by the firm at Carn Brea. *It has* been proposed that as soon as the machinery was installed, to start training 30 girls of school-leaving age and perhaps a little older, in the Green-lane property.   20/6/1946

Challenge Accepted

The challenge recently published in the *West Briton* by Mr. C.H. Allen, of Hayle, to race his well-known prize-winning donkey, Star, on a mile grass track with any cyclist in Devon or Cornwall, has been accepted by Mr. Charles Rule, of Falmouth.

Mr. Rule is a founder member of West Cornwall Cycling Club, which he claims to be the oldest of its kind in the county. The race will be run in Redruth Recreation Ground on ...July 11th.   20/6/1946

Mine Ashore At Newquay

Two Newquay boatmen, Messers. D. Todman and E. Hoare, saw a mine floating in Newquay Bay, yesterday morning, and reported it to the authorities. People were warned to quit Towan Beach and Promenade. The progress of the mine was watched with interest and suspense by hundreds, and it came to rest on sand between two large rocks not far from the Island, having just missed striking the Bothwicks Rocks. A house on the cliff above had to be evacuated. A mine disposal squad from Devonport arrived in the afternoon, and successfully dealt with the mine.   20/6/1946

English Draughts Champion

Mr. W.E. Glasson, of St Austell, first Cornish winner of the English Draughts Championship, has also won the Cornish title for the eleventh time.   27/6/1946

Backward Hay Harvest

The hay harvest is very backward this year and only a few isolated cases the crop has been cut. Normally hay-harvesting is in full swing by Midsummer Day, and almost completed by the second week in July. The crop promises to yield well in most places, and farmers are waiting for better weather to ripen it, with a fair prospect of saving in good conditions before embarking on full-scale cutting.   27/6/1946

N.F.S. As Water-Carriers

Members of Penzance N.F.S., on Tuesday, took 2,800 gallons of water to Mr. T.N. Phillips' house at Allwynds, Perranuthoe, and 2,500 gallons to two cottages... Mr. Phillips had had to fetch water by horse and cart up to Tuesday. His water tanks had not been full for two years, and the rain at the end of May and beginning of June only half-filled them. In the case of the two cottages, workmen were repairing defects in the supply from the roof to the rain water tank.   27/6/1946

Commando Ridge

Carn Galva, near Gurnards Head, *has been* renamed Commando Ridge, where many Commandos received training in rock climbing for their hazardous operations. 27/6/1946

Bread Rationing

On or after July 21st, 1946, bread, flour, cakes, buns and scones will be rationed in one scheme and measured by BREAD UNITS (BU's). This will allow you as much freedom of choice as possible. BU values will be as follows:

BREAD	1 small loaf (14ozs.)	2 BU's
	1 large loaf (1 lb. 12ozs.)	4 BU's
FLOUR	1 lb.	3 BU's
	3 lbs.	9 BU's

CAKES, BUNS, SCONES: ½ lb   1 BU
                              1 lb   2 BU's

You can spend your Bread Units where you choose, on what you choose of these flour foods, and when you choose within each 4-week period, but remember they have to last for the whole period.

There then follows the number of BU's allowed for each person.

Children under 1	2 BU's
child aged 1-5	4 BU's
child aged 5 to 11	4 BU's
adolescents, 11 to 18	12 BU's
normal adults	9 BU's
expectant mothers	11 BU's
manual workers (woman)	12 BU's
manual worker, (man)	19 BU's.

4/7/1946

In City And Village

Sir – I was greatly surprised on visiting Truro one evening last week to find the streets illuminated, in contravention of the advice tendered to local authorities by the Ministry of Fuel and Power to discontinue public lighting until the end of August in the interest of fuel economy. What, however, occasioned me even greater amazement was, on passing through Chacewater at 11.15 p.m., to find all the electric street lights still burning and not a soul to be seen anywhere.

                        Yours truly, Economist.   4/7/1946

Admiralty Gifts

Moored side by side off the Prince of Wales Pier, Falmouth, two camouflage-grey painted motor torpedo boats, Nos. 610 and 617, each 115 ft. long, have aroused the interest of sightseers, but more so of the youthful "crews" who possess them. M.T.B. 610 has been presented by the Admiralty as a county training ship for the Scouts and Sea Scouts. M.T.B. 617 is a gift from the Admiralty to Falmouth Sea Cadet Corps., and, unofficially but enthusiastically there is keen competition between rival youths to fit out their vessels in true ship-shape fashion.   4/7/1946

Penryn Adopts Points System For Houses

A point system for letting of council houses was adopted by Penryn Town Council, on Tuesday, for which the main allocation of points are to be made being: Serviceman's widow, 10; Serviceman and wife, 6; badly overcrowded families, 6; parents suffering from tuberculosis, 8; applicant and/or wife born in the borough, 5; married young people without homes, 5; house destroyed by enemy action, 4; widows, excepting Service widows and old age pensioners, 8; disability through war service, 4.   4/7/1946

A Rare Inquest

Inquests of this kind are very rare, and this was the first to be held in Cornwall for at least 50 years. The late Mr. Edward Boase, the coroner was ill, and so his partner, Mr. Bennetts, who was the deputy-coroner, sat in with a jury in the Wesleyan Schoolroom, at Nancledra, on January 1st, 1932, to hold an inquest on eight gold articles laid out before them. They had been unearthed on December 11th, 1931, by Mr. Ernest Thomas Berryman, a farm labourer, who was digging up an old bank in a croft at Almalveor Farm, Towednack, when he came across what he thought were "bits of old iron", caked in mud. A St. Ives jeweller thought

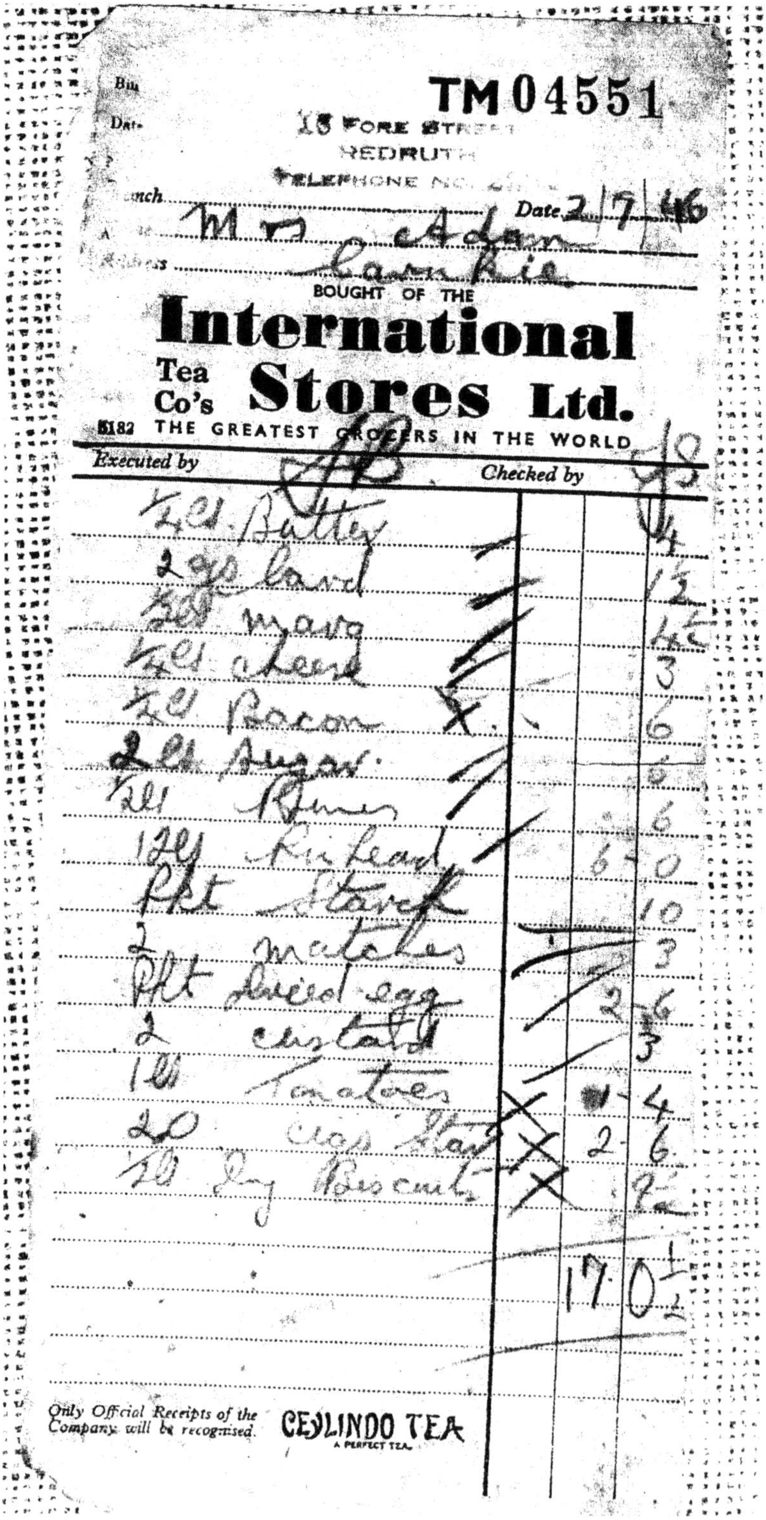

13 FORE STREET
REDRUTH
TELEPHONE NO.

Bill
Date

Branch

Date 2/7/46

Mrs Adam
Carnkie

Address

BOUGHT OF THE

International
Tea Co's Stores Ltd.

5182 THE GREATEST GROCERS IN THE WORLD

Executed by	Checked by		
½ lb. Butter			4
2 go lard			1/2
mayo			4½
½ lb cheese			3
½ lb Bacon			6
2 lb Sugar			6
½ lb Beans			6
1 lb Ptea		6	0
Pkt Starch			10
2 matches			3
Pkt dried egg		2	6
2 custard			3
1 lb Tomatoes			4
20 cig stars		2	6
½ lb dry Biscuits			1½
		17	0½

Only Official Receipts of the Company will be recognised.   **CEYLINDO TEA** A PERFECT TEA they were brass until tests ascertained they were gold.

Two of the pieces were torques and the other articles were raw material used for making things, or used as currency. They are now in the British Museum, and replicas displayed in the museum at Penzance.   11/7/1946

More Clothing Coupons

Good news for West Cornwall inshore fishermen is that from 1st August they will be eligible for the same number of supplementary clothing coupons as deep-sea fishermen receive. This will enable them to buy protective clothing.   11/7/1946

A Tidal Wave

Parts of Penryn were flooded and a number of small craft were washed adrift in the Falmouth and Helford waters by a tidal wave which caused considerable damage between Torbay and The Land's End during Wednesday night. High tide was at 9.30 p.m. at Falmouth, but, about two hours after that, the sea suddenly made an unexpected rising of another five feet and reached a higher level than any normal tide.

… In the Penryn River, craft were thrown up above high water mark, and a section of a tank landing craft broke adrift. In Falmouth Harbour, several craft went adrift, including a motor mine sweeper, a trawler and some yachts.   11/7/1946

Market Day Travel

When cheap day fares on the railways come into operation on August 1st, cheap day tickets on market days in towns with a population of 10,000 or over in the West

John Knill Ceremony near St. Ives. Fiddler John Care with children singing "Old Hundredth".
25/7/1946

Country will be available to Camborne and Truro (market days, Wednesday), Penzance (Thursday), and St Austell and Redruth (Friday). At stations within 20 miles of those towns, tickets will be issued on market days stated. Specimen fares are:-

        To Camborne – Penzance (2s 5d), St Ives (2s 1d), Helston (2s 1d), Truro (2s 4d).
        To Truro – Hayle (3s 4d), Redruth (1s 9d), Falmouth (2s 1d), St Austell (2s 7d).
        To Penzance – Redruth (3s), Hayle (1s 4d), St Ives (1s 9d).
        To St Austell – Lostwithiel (1s 8d), Doublebois (3s 3d).   11/7/1946

Cow Has "Quads"
Having given birth to four calves, on Wednesday, a Devon cow, owned by Mrs. Tregenan, Tregoweth, Mylor, has become famous for an extremely rare occurrence in the cattle breeding world. This is her third time of calving. The "quads" consist of three heifers and a bull, all are doing well.   18/7/1946

What! No Pasties?
"What is to become of the Cornish pasty after tomorrow when the rationing of flour and bread commence, I very much wonder. I trust we are not going to see a temporary eclipse of this famous product of the Duchy", observed Mrs. D. Lee, Bonithon, Praa Sands, on opening, on Saturday, the third annual exhibition of horticultural and home produce and handicrafts, organised by Breage and District Women's Institute.   25/7/1946

Bus Shelters
The Highways Committee reported to Camborne – Redruth Urban Council, on Monday, their decision asking the Great Western Railway Company to provide shelters for waiting 'bus passengers on their private road outside Redruth Railway Station.
This road continued to be a private road for many years and was closed on Christmas day. 1/8/1946

Trencom Hill As Gift To Nation
Trencom Hill, a well-known 500 feet-high landmark, near St. Ives, which has been presented to the National Trust by the owner, Colonel G.L. Tyingham, of Trevethoe, Lelant, as a memorial to Cornish people who gave their lives in the wars of 1914-1918 and 1939-1945.   1/8/1946

Replacing Railings And Ironwork
Penryn Town Council, on Tuesday, decided to ask Mr. E.M. King, M.P. for Penryn–Falmouth, to put before Parliament, a request that steps be taken nationally to replace railings and ornamental ironwork removed during the war for scrap, or to compensate property-owners by payment and remove restrictions so that they can make replacements privately.   1/8/1946

A New Problem
"In former times a problem was created by so many children were under-weight. Today the position has been reversed", remarked Dr. (Mrs.) E.M. Macdonald (Roskear), judge of a baby show, which drew 20 entries, at Illogan Parish Church fete in the Rectory grounds, on Thursday.   1/8/1946

Rodeo At Mabe
Bare-back riding on untamed Dartmoor ponies provided riders and spectators with plenty of thrills at Mabe, on Saturday, when a Penryn sailor and two Mawnan Smith girls were among the winners for staying longest on the bounding diminutive bronchos.   8/8/1946

Lady Tremayne, Capt. Warren-Wren (Camp Commander), Sir John Tremayne, and Mr. A. L. Rowse at the International Youth Camp at Heligan.　　　　　*16/8/1946*

Cyclist's Ride To London

R.J. Coad, a racing member of the West Cornwall Cycling Club, has cycled form Launceston to London, a distance of 216 miles, in 13 hours, eight minutes, with only three stops during the journey. Mr. Coad had, on the previous day, competed in a 25-mile time trial, in which he clocked one hour, 10 minutes, 47 seconds. Afterwards he rode from near Truro to Launceston, leaving for London at 5 a.m. next morning. The return journey, owing to an unfavourable wind, took 14½ hours, but, nevertheless, was a very creditable performance.　　　　　*8/8/1946*

Drama Of The Sea

The crew of ten of the s.s. Kedah were rescued as the ship *a twin-screwed steamer of 2,55 tons* was being driven towards the rocks at St. Agnes during Mondays gale, after two lifeboats had been launched to go to her aid in heavy seas. The smaller St. Ives lifeboat was beaten back, but the Padstow men came down the coast, and though their boat was buffeted against the steamer side, they effected a very gallant rescue... The heavy sea was too much for the St. Ives lifeboat, and after a three hour fight she was forced to return to her station. Meanwhile, St. Agnes L.S.A. team had been called out, and they stood watching the Kedah drifting towards them. Under Coastguard W. Sparrock, they were ready to fire a rocket line across the vessel at first opportunity.

The crew were eventually taken off by the Padstow lifeboat.   15/8/1946

In The Roar Of The Cornish Sea
Riding the long Atlantic surges on a surf-board is a popular form of amusement at Porthmeor Beach, St. Ives, where many visitors are enjoying the invigorating Cornish air for the first time for many years.   15/8/1946

On Carn Brea Slope
For more than a century Methodism has been established at Tregagorran, Illogan, on the slope of Carn Brea Hill. The present chapel, which it is claimed, stands near the site of the cottage in which Richard Trevithic was born, was built about 80 years ago, and the adjoining schoolroom in 1908.   22/8/1946

Falmouth Commemorates Castle Epic
Wearing red cassocks of their church of royal foundation, choristers of Falmouth Parish Church of King Charles the Martyr sang Spring-Rice's beautiful anthem, "I vow to thee, my country", on the battlements of 400 year old Pendennis Castle on Saturday. The occasion was a ceremony of remembrance of the epic resistance by Sir John Arundell and his Royalist supporters during the six-month siege by the Parliamentary Forces in 1646.

22/8/1946

Farm Survey
The National Farm Survey, compiled by the Ministry of Agriculture, shows that Cornwall has 11,000 agricultural holdings of five acres and upwards, the fourth largest number of any administrative county in England. These farms have an aggregate of 613,000 acres of crops and grass. Only 14% of the holdings are equipped with electricity, 24% a seasonal shortage of water, and 16% have no source of water supply to their fields. All three percentages show the position in Cornwall to be inferior in national average.   5/9/1946

The "Mock Suns"
A most unusual phenomena was observed at Penzance, on Thursday morning. Mr. C.J. Baker, the borough meteorological officer, saw an incomplete sun halo and on the edge of it were three "mock suns". Mock suns, which take the form of blobs of rainbow-coloured light, are rarely seen and when they do appear they usually consist of a group of four. They are caused by the reflection of the sun on ice particles in the sky, and usually means a further period of bad weather.   5/9/1946

The Well Of St Euny
An antiquity of national interest, and its special responsibility of the people of Redruth, is the holy well dedicated to St. Eunius, the patron saint of Redruth parish. This ancient structure stands in picturesque surroundings at the foot of Carn Brea, with the old tower of the parish church nestling in trees on one side, and the stark, imposing background of the hill on the other. It lies in a valley close to the road leading from Redruth Rectory to the village of Carn Brea. Through that valley, and under and across the roadway near the well, there flows a lively tin-stream, the likely site of a ford of stepping stones from which the name "Redruth" (Red Ford) may have originated.

5/9/1946

Giant Onions

Mr. E. Kessel, Trevenner, Marazion, has grown some very large onions, one remarkable specimen being 1 lb. 7 ozs. in weight, and 17 inches in circumference.   12/9/1946

A Great Day

"Where are the plums?" was a question asked by many of the thousands of people from all parts of the West, South and Mid-Cornwall who thronged the streets of Helston, on Monday, for the annual Harvest or plum fair. There was scarcely a plum to be seen in the town, whereas in pre-war times large quantities were on sale. Missing, too, were "standings" of fruit, sweets and confectionery the whole length of one side of Coinage-hall-street.   12/9/1946

Gorsedd Again — First Since 1938

> "Since there is Peace,
> Let us then proceed.
> Before the Sun,
> The Eve of Day,
> The Gorsedd is opened".

Spoken in old Cornish, those words by Grand Bard Morden (Mr. R. Morton Nance) were the preamble to a most impressive Cornish Gorsedd at Perran Round, on Saturday. The Horn of the Nation had been sounded to the four winds by Tan Tyvarow (Bard F.B. Cargreen) calling attention of all Cornwall to the assembly of the Bards…This was the most successful ceremony since 1928 *when it was revised*. Oldest Bard present was 91 year old, Mr. Bray, of St. Kew.   12/9/1946

First Handbell Peal

Ringing history for the Truro Diocesan Guild of Ringers was made on Wednesday, when the first handbell peal ever rung in Cornwall was successfully brought round in Carbis Bay Church in two hours and thirty-four minutes. The peal was one of Bob Major, 5,040 changes.   12/9/1946

Cracked Eggs

Sir – As a reader of The *West Briton*, I was very interested in the case of the baker who used cracked eggs for sandwiches. May I ask what becomes of such eggs sent to the packing stations? What are they used for? Who has them? It is three weeks since I had eggs from the shop where I am registered, and a few cracked ones would be better than none provided they were fresh.

                    Housewife.   26/9/1946

Twice The village It Was

The village of Pengagon, Camborne, has been more than doubled by the erection by Messrs. G.E. Wallis Ltd., for the Ministry of Works of 50 pre-fabricated houses, all but six of which are now occupied at a weekly rental of 15s., including rates… There are two good-sized bedrooms, two excellent living rooms (*one of which served as a kitchen-diner*), and a bathroom. Hot and cold water is laid on and heating is by both electricity and from an anthracite fire in the living room. As soon as supplies are available, a refrigerator will be installed in each kitchen.   26/9/1946

100 M.P.H. Gales

The worst September gale for 37 years hit Cornwall at about mid-day on Friday, reaching at times a velocity of 100 miles an hour. From all over the county came reports of stripped roofs, chimneys wrenched off, fallen trees (in many cases blocking roads), the hurling down of the already not very extensive apple and plum crops, and the blowing about of corn mous… The gale was accompanied by very heavy rain and the atmosphere was extremely wintery. 26/9/1946

Culdrose Aerodrome
Described by Mr. W. Arnold-Forster as the worst injury ever inflicted by the Service Departments in Cornwall, Culdrose Aerodrome, near Helston, was the cause of profound anxiety and dismay… It appeared that the matters were worse than had been supposed. Nine or ten valuable farms had been sacrificed, as well as hundreds of acres of rich agricultural land. No planning interests had been taken into consideration.
3/10/1946

"Squatters"
With a waiting list of 650 applicants for the 130 houses and twelve flats which comprise the first part of their post-war housing programme, Falmouth Town Council find themselves, today, with a precipitated housing problem which involves the Admiralty, the Home Office, and the principles of law and order, …for, during the weekend, several families have followed the example set by up-country semi-homeless and overcrowded families and have become "squatters". *They had broken into the disused former United States Naval camp between Beacon and Dracaena-avenue.* 3/10/1946

The Royal Cornwall
The decision of the Royal Cornwall Agricultural Association to revive the show in 1947 on a date to be fixed so as to facilitate the visit of a very distinguished visitor, was reported to Truro City Council, on Tuesday. The probable dates are June 25th and 26th or July 9th and 10th. *It was to be held at Tregurra, Truro.* 10/10/1946

Diphtheria At Falmouth
Details concerning an outbreak of diphtheria in Falmouth were forthcoming at Falmouth Town Council, on Tuesday, when Mr. A. Hey (the sanitary inspector) reported that there were 15 cases including two notified on Monday. 10/10/1946

Mosquitto Crashes
A Mosquitto aircraft crashed at Tresean, Cubert, on Tuesday morning. The pilot and navigator were killed. The 'plane struck the electric cable, cutting off the electricity. Narrowly missing some cottages, it came in collision with an implement house, owned by Mr. H. Reed, and damaged the machinery and struck a cow… injuring it so badly, that it had to be killed. 10/10/1946

Film-making At Falmouth
Well-known star Michael Redgrave, will feature in a film *The Man Within*, which Gainsborough Pictures anticipate making in part at Falmouth, and it is possible that the schooner Volant, which set out on a voyage from Belfast to Australia with a share-holder crew and ended her journey at Falmouth, may be used in the film. 10/10/1946

Oil From Pilchards
Preliminary rests in the reduction of pilchards for oil for the manufacture of margarine having proved successful, representatives from the Ministry of Food came to Newlyn,

New Housing Estate. Mrs. Blatchford receiving the key of the front door at New Housing Estate, St. Austell. *21/10/1946*

on Thursday, to discuss with fishermen the price at which they are prepared to sell pilchards to the Ministry to enable experiment to be carried out on a much larger scale.

17/10/1946

For London Zoo

Bound from Mombasa to London with the largest single consignment of animals and birds ever shipped for the London Zoo, the s.s. Urlana put in at Falmouth, on Tuesday, for engine repairs. Noah of this modern Ark is Mr. C.S. Webb of London Zoo staff… who has brought from Africa 150 animals and 150 birds to replace the Zoo's stock after the war years… Decks were crowed with crates. Giraffes extended unexpectedly friendly greetings with gentle licks on the heads. There were lions, leopards, cheetahs, chimpanzees, delightful docile antelopes, hyenas, porcupines with blue and yellow quills, zebra, a baby rhinoceros valued at £600, and birds of all hues, varying from a giant ostrich to some smaller than an English wren. *17/10/1946*

Mining Scenes For Film

Mr. F.R. Mitchell, West Trewirgie, Redruth, is a member of the staff of the School of Metalliferous Mining, Camborne, and joint secretary of the Cornish Institute of

Engineers, acted as technical advisor, and supplied data and photographs of old mining scenes, in connection with the making of the film *Hungry Hill*, based on Daphne du Maurier's book. It deals with the importation of miners into Ireland. 24/10/1946

Peal Of Eight

For 400 years, according to ancient records, the bells of St. Gluvias, Penryn, have sent out their calls to the faithful pealing across the peaceful countryside. The tradition of ringing is being carried on with girls… assisting the male ringers. An old document states that an inventory of church goods taken in the reign of Edward V1, 1549, to be seen at the Public Records Office, London, mentions "St Gluvias Church – itm—Three Bells in Ye Tower". The present six bells were hung in 1808… One new bell is being given by the Webber family… in memory of the late Mr. Ernest Webber, and the other is being given by Mr. J. Tripp. Cost of each bell is about £60. *"itm" – item* 31/10/1946

Advertisement

Goerings Pride

Crossing the Goss Moor at 80 m.p.h. – a faster speed was not deemed safe in such a short run – Capt. J.F. Thurlby, who is acting as hon. transport officer, demonstrated to representatives of the Press, who were passengers, the capabilities of the extensively bullet-splattered Mercedes Benz car, once the pride of Hermann Goering, when the vehicle was on the final stage of its run from Glasgow to Truro, on Thursday afternoon. 4/11/1946

Remembrance

The French Government arranged for floral tributes to be placed on the graves of members of the Free French Forces who are buried in this country, and last Friday wreaths were placed on graves in Falmouth, Helston and Illogan. 7/11/1946

Billy Bray's Chair

Kerley Downs ("Three Eyes") Methodist Chapel, which was built by Billy Bray, the famous Cornish evangelist and stalwart of the former Bible Christian denomination, with the help of his little son, will shortly contain a direct link with its founder in the form of an ordinary table-sized mahogany chair with a large oak seat. The chair has a tallish carved back, and on the seat is cut in perfect lettering, "Billy Bray, Baldhu, 1839". It is believed this was actually Billy's workmanship. Written on a piece of paper stuck on the back of the chair is, "Bought at William Jory's Marine Store sale, Truro, 1869". Billy Bray who was born at Twelveheads in 1794, died on May 25th, 1868. 7/11/1946

Huer's Trumpet On Dump

One of the old huer's trumpets used by the huers in Newquay's pilchard fishing days, was last week found on a refuse dump in Porth. It was marked with the name of

Clemens and belonged to the Fly-Seining Co. The finder was Mr. Norman T. Pender, of Fairview-terrace, Newquay. He has refused several offers from would-be purchasers.

7/11/1946

1901 Steam Limousine

Yesterday, in the Redruth district, a 1901 steam car puffed merrily alng the highway, causing folks to look a second time. Owner by Com. B. Crossley-Meates, R.N. (retired) and Mrs. Crossley-Meates, of Machan, Manaccan, the antique vehicle proceeded from Messrs. W.E. Old's coach-building works at Pool to Helston railway station to be transported to London for the London-Brighton "old crock" race… It is a two-cylinder "White" limousine carrying a driver and three passengers, who entered the vehicle by a door at the rear. A spare wheel on the roof is reached by using a collapsible ladder.

14/11/1946

Advertisement

Redruth's New Industry

Messrs. John Heathcott and Co., lace and textile manufacturers, of Tiverton, have transferred their branch establishment from the council building in Station-hill, Redruth, to much ampler accommodation at the former W.A.A.F. Station near Portreath, which is being occupied by three firms.

21/11/1946

Falmouth Man Suggests New Industry

Mr. A.V. Baker, a well-known Falmouth business man, has been in communication with the Ministry of Food on the possibilities of a new industry in Cornwall by extracting the gelatine content from certain types of seaweed for various trade uses.

21/11/1946

From Sea To Table

A new venture in Cornish fishing is being made at Falmouth by eight ex-Service, former Army, Navy and R.A.F. officers, who are acquiring several Admiralty fishing vessels and have formed a company to undertake deep-sea fishing off Cornish shores. Modernised ideas in packing and marketing are contemplated by the ex-officers, who are now negotiating to secure suitable foreshore premises as a trading base… Proposals of the ex-Service officers is to do deep-sea trawling and seining, and for this work the craft they are securing are ideal… The proposals include an icing plant. As soon as the fish are brought aboard the trawlers they will be iced immediately. Ashore they will be packed in small containers such as those used… during the war for cold storage of foodstuffs.

21/11/1946

Are You Married ?

Sir – Why are married ex-Service men being victimised? Why are we told that the Government are alarmed at the decreasing birth-rate, but those of us who are married and have two or more children seem to be on a "sellers" market as far as jobs are concerned. I have applied for numerous vacancies since being released, and seven out of ten interviews have started with the question, "Are you married?"

I can fully understand the necessity of employers cutting down the expenses of the present time, but am at a loss to know why married boys who did the job of "Jerry punching" should suffer most. Can any reader suggest a cure?

E.S. Tucker.
19, Vogue-terrace, St. Day   28/11/1946

Eggs Bacon Fats
More of them from your kitchen scraps

If 250 housewives regularly contribute their kitchen scraps they would provide sufficient feeding stuffs to feed 500 poultry or 30 pigs for one week. This shows how important it is to put your potato and apple peelings, table scraps and vegetable leaves in the nearest pig bin.

Do NOT include orange, lemon, banana or grapefruit skins. And no salt, soap or soda, please.   Issued by the Board of Trade.

2/12/1946

Camborne "B.R."

Reported decision by the Finance Committee to close Camborne British Restaurant at the end of the Christmas holidays and to consider further at its next meeting the future of Redruth British Restaurant, was confirmed by Camborne-Redruth Urban District

B.U.'s being delivered to Eustice's, bakers.   *December 1946*

Council, on Thursday. 5/12/1946

For Falmouth Boys

A number of free allotments may be available to Falmouth boys in the next few days, together with free seeds for planting. Provision is being made for this by Falmouth Allotments and Garden Society, which took over six acres of newly, freshly-ploughed land at Old-hill, on Saturday, to replace plots lost at Beacon through Falmouth Town Council's acquisition for building. Purpose of the free facilities to boys is to foster gardening interest among the younger generation. 5/12/1946

Gale Warnings

A short time ago the fishermen in West Cornwall made representation to the West Cornwall Fishermen's Council as to the inadequacy of gale warnings broadcast by the B.B.C… *A letter was received from the West Regional Programme Director of the B.B.C.:-*
"I am glad to be able to tell you that, as a result of your representations, we are starting at once a new gale warning service on the West Home Service (307 and 217 metres). From today onwards we shall broadcast immediately before the 1 p.m. news any warning reaching us during the morning. We shall be covering the entire area from West Channel to Beachy Head, including the Channel Islands, the Isle of Wight, and also the Bristol Channel. 5/12/1946

Stole Rowing Boat

Because he wanted to go to sea, 20-year-old Robert McArthur, of 9, Appleby-street, Glasgow North, hitch-hiked from Southampton to Falmouth, stole an eleven-foot rowing-boat in the early hours of Monday morning, rigged a sail from one of the paddles and a piece of cloth, and sailed out of Falmouth Bay in an attempt to contact an American cargo ship which he knew would be passing Falmouth about that time.
McArthur and the rowing-boat were washed ashore near St. Anthony Lighthouse, where the boat capsized, and McArthur managed to scramble ashore… The Magistrates (Paymaster-Lt. Com. R.W. Thorn and Mr. G.R. Ennor) released accused with a fine of 5s., and advised him to leave the district. He said he was returning to Southampton immediately. — Supt. Morcumb paid the five shillings. 5/12/1946

Lifetime In Shipping

From the days of globe-voyaging sailing ships to the peak period of shipping transport in the war just ended, the name of "Mr. Chapman" was known along the Falmouth waterways, for Mr. George Henry Chapman, aged 79, of 22, Trelawney-road, whose funeral took place at Falmouth Cemetery, last week, had a unique association with the shipping of the port, and was known to sea captains and ships' officers the world over. At 14 he started as an office boy with Messrs. G.C. Fox and Co., shipping agents, and a year later he was among the first in Falmouth to use a telephone, when Messrs. Fox installed the first instrument in 1883. Those were the days of windjammers and sailing craft. 5/12/1946

Evacuee's Gift

A pleasant ceremony took place at Manaccan on Sunday, when a beautiful barometer was presented to Manaccan and St. Anthony parishioners by Mr. A.A. Edwards, on behalf of the Tottenham and Bristol evacuees billeted in the parishes during the war. Mr. R. Cannicott (chairman of Manaccan Parish Council), who presided, said he believed

Manaccan and St. Anthony were the first parishes in Cornwall to be honoured in that
way. 12/12/1946

"Best In England"

Mr. A.G. Street, a well-known agriculturalist, who recently attended the annual
ploughing and hedging demonstration – arranged by Camborne Farmers' Union, at the
close of an article in *The Farmers' Weekly* writes;- "By the way, before I forget — I want to
pay a tribute to Cornwall's roads. I have been doing a lot of road travel lately, and as a
result have to place it on record that the surface, sign-posting, and verge tidiness,
Cornish roads are the best in England. Maybe this county's roads did not have to carry
so much war traffic as those in other districts; but, when travelling west by car, what a
relief it is to get out of Devon!" 12/12/1946

To Repair Bomb Damage

To repair damage done by blast from German bombs, which affected the roof and other
portions of the building and to replace fabric affected by dry-rot, members of St. Mary's
Roman Catholic Church, Falmouth, held a Christmas sale of work yesterday. …Bombs
which demolished houses in Kimberly-place considerably shook the church with its fine
tower and spire. 12/12/1946

XMAS CHEER
One Minute News

**43 tons of this fruit was for
Rowe and Co.**

**Fruit — 89 tons of fresh fruit, and
37,836 bags of mail are due at
Southampton on Friday from
America**

The choicest variety of fruit since 1939 by direct importations.

2,000 c/s Oregon Beurre Bosc Pears	(landed, see above)
2,000 c/s Californian White Nellis Pears	(due Avonmouth Dec 18th)
300 lugs Californian Grapes	(due Newcastle Dec 20th)
1,000 Mandarines	(landed)
1,000 bags Dutch onions	(landed)
1,000 bags Dutch onions	(to arrive)

Ministry of Food Allocation

1,000 boats Canary Tomatoes	(expected)
1,090 c/s South African Oranges	
1,163 boxes Canadian Eating Apples	

A Banana Distribution and the usual lines.

ROWE and Co., Redruth 280/281

St. Austell 577 Falmouth 380 Penzance 886/568
12/12/1946

Workers' Buses

The Western National Omnibus Co., Ltd., was criticised at a meeting of the Camborne-
Redruth Trades council, on Thursday, for "lack of immediate co-operation" in provision
of transport facilities for certain industrial workers. Mr. W.H. Verran, (hon sec.), reported
that he had asked the company for the immediate starting of early morning and evening
workers' 'bus service from Camborne via Tuckingmill, Pool and Paynter's Lane End to
the disused W.A.A.F. Station at Bridge… Some girls, coming from as far a way as Praze,

Army cooks at Bodmin Barracks with their Christmas cakes.   *December 1946*

had to pay nearly five shillings weekly for transport.   12/12/1946

Cart Colts Wanted

We are pleased to buy any quantity of colts and prime quality fat horses for human consumption. All horses guaranteed slaughtered at our local slaughter-house. Our prices cannot be beaten in the country. We shall be pleased to buy your colts and horses per cwt., live-weight, on an official weighbridge.

Distance No Object
Haynes and Co., Helston
Phone: Helston 21 and Mullion 213

12/12/1946

Advertisement

28 h.p. Dodge Jeeps, Large-type Command Cars, ex-M.O.S., 4-wheel drive. Eminently suitable farmers. Capable of driving through muddiest of conditions.
     Price £195.   Lanyon Motors Ltd., Redruth.   Phone: 286

12/12/1946

Send This Combined Greeting and Gift

Solve your problem of Christmas present and greeting cards this way. Get as many of these free coloured Gift Cards as you need. In the spaces inside put any number you like of 6d., or 2/6 or 5/- Savings Stamps and the gift is ready.

National Savings Gift Cards

Obtainable from any Post Office, Trustee Savings Bank, Savings Centre or Group.

16/12/1946

Premier Fat Stock Award

A South Devon steer, owned by Mr. Spencer Jacka, of Truhall Manor, Helston,… won the Presidents' Cup and The West Briton Challenge Cup for the best beast at Truro Fat Stock Show.

19/12/1946

Rang In Own Birthday Peal

Mr. Samuel Quintrell, of 27, West-street, St. Columb, celebrated his 91st birthday on Friday. He rang in his own birthday peal in the evening, and rang again on Sunday. Mr. Quintrell has been a ringer for about 75 years, and captain of the tower at St. Columb for over 50 years.

19/12/1946

Kindness And Gratitude

The following story was told by Mrs. G.H. Johnstone at the annual meeting of the Friends of the Hospital at Truro, on Thursday. Part of the money we gave to the Samaritan Fund went for pocket-money to a patient during his convalescence. He was a young boy who had formerly been at an approved school, and he was given £1 – 5s. After his convalescence, and from his first week's wages, he sent back 10s. 19/12/1946

Citrons For King

Carefully packed and with an appropriate Christmas greeting, selected citrons from a large tree growing in the open at Falmouth's Rosehill-gardens were despatched, on Friday, by the Mayor, (Ald. W.A. Lamb) as a Christmas gesture to H.M. the King to show that "Falmouth can grow it". The fruit were picked by the Mayor in a prime ripe state, months to ripen, and were golden yellow. They had reached this mature stage after careful attention of Mr. T.C. Rowe, the corporation gardener. Citrons take 15 months to ripen, and the tree had withstood two winters in the open. 26/12/1946

Christmas Spirit

Falmouth's Christmas has never been complete without the docks workers' choir singing their carols in the main streets when leaving work at mid-day on Christmas eve. And today, in their soiled working clothes, straight from the shipyard, they wil be repeating the practice – stopping at various points to tender familiar carols in tuneful harmony.

26/12/1946

Marooned In Lighthouse

Two B.B.C. men, Mr. Edward Ward and Mr. Stanley Cooms, have spent 10 days on the Bishop Rock lighthouse, off the Isles of Scilly, where they arrived to broadcast for three minutes on Christmas day. Bad weather prevented their return. 30/12/1946